BEST-LOVED SAINTS

*Inspiring Biographies of Popular Saints
for Young Catholics and Adults*

**By
Rev. Lawrence G. Lovasik, S.V.D.**
Divine Word Missionary

CATHOLIC BOOK PUBLISHING CORP.
New Jersey

NIHIL OBSTAT: Daniel V. Flynn, J.C.D.
Censor Librorum

IMPRIMATUR: ✠ Joseph T. O'Keefe, D.D.
Administrator, Archdiocese of New York

(T-160)

ISBN 978-0-89942-160-5

FOREWORD

AS material possessions and personal ambitions fail to satisfy, more and more people are turning to the life lived in Christ—the spiritual life, a holy life. We can learn what it means to live a holy life from those who heroically dedicated themselves to imitating Christ—the saints.

Based on authentic historical records, this book contains warmly human portraits of men and women whose faith, courage, and love exemplify the life of a Christian saint. They lived in every age, in every part of the earth, in every kind of Christian community. They were ordinary people whose words and actions testified to their belief in Jesus Christ.

The heart of this book lies in the personal narratives, which confirm that not all saints' lives are the same. They are shaped by their times, by individual traits of personality, by trials faced and endured. What they have in common is their devotion to the living Word of God, Jesus Christ, who said of himself: "I am the way, the truth, and the life." That is what makes every one of these dramatic stories a perfect vehicle for meditation and inspiration to help us imitate these, our wonderful brothers and sisters in Christ, in our own small way.

I have grouped these stories in chronological order so that the reader may appreciate the growth of spiritual life in the Church over many centuries. May these examples of Christian virtue serve as an inspiration to us in our own day-to-day striving for holiness.

Father Lawrence G. Lovasik, S.V.D.

CONTENTS

Mary, Queen of All Saints . 7
Joseph 10
Joachim and Anne 15
Paul of Tarsus 18
Stephen, First Martyr 28
Cecilia 31
Agnes 35
Lawrence 38
Jerome 41
Augustine of Hippo 44
Patrick 50
Leo the Great 53
Dymphna 57
Boniface 61
Cyril and Methodius 64
Bernard 68
Dominic 71
Francis of Assisi 74
Clare 80
Anthony of Padua 83
Bonaventure 86
Thomas Aquinas 89
Bridget of Sweden 93
Catherine of Siena 96
Angela Merici 100
Thomas More 103

Ignatius Loyola 107
John of God 111
Francis Xavier 115
Charles Borromeo 118
John of the Cross 121
Vincent de Paul 124
Teresa of Jesus 128
Robert Bellarmine 132
Camillus of Lellis 135
Jane Frances de Chantal 139
Francis de Sales 142
Aloysius Gonzaga 145
Martin de Porres 148
Rose of Lima 152
Margaret Mary Alacoque 155
Alphonsus Liguori 158
Elizabeth Bayley Seton 162
John Bosco 168
John Neumann 171
Pius X 174
Marie Bernadette
   Soubirous 177
Frances Xavier Cabrini ... 181
Thérèse of the Child Jesus 184
Maria Goretti 187

MARY, QUEEN OF ALL SAINTS

MARY, the Mother of God and our Mother, is the Queen of all saints because she made the most diligent use of the rich treasure of grace which God granted to her. Her thoughts were always occupied in learning to know and praise God; her heart loved Him above all things. She zealously accepted every inspiration to good. Thus sanctifying grace was wondrously increased in her soul.

Mary was no more than a teenager when she was called to her special mission by God. Her home was in Nazareth, a village in Galilee that was so unimportant, it hadn't been mentioned in the Bible before her time. Like most Jews of her time, Mary and the others in her village were poor. They were simple people who lived plain lives and worked hard.

Romans had occupied the land of the Jews and the people were hoping and praying that a Messiah would come to rescue them from their oppressors. But they were looking for someone who looked like a mighty king. When God sent a Messiah who was like His people, poor, He chose Mary as Jesus' mother because she too was one of the poor. She was someone willing to be the servant of God.

Because she was full of grace, Mary also excelled in every virtue much more than every other saint. All the traits of Jesus were expressed in her as faithfully as they could be expressed in any creature. Because of her fullness of grace and the splendor of her virtues, she was raised above all the saints; she is their Queen.

7

Mary was raised above all the saints in glory. Chosen from among all human beings, she sits on a throne of surpassing splendor. Scripture can be applied to her: "She shall be admired in the holy assembly, and in the multitude of the elect she shall have praise; and among the blessed she shall be blessed" (Sir 24:3).

As she surpasses all saints in choosing a virtuous and meritorious life, so Mary stands higher than all the elect in receiving glory and reward. After God there is no greater bliss for the blessed in heaven than to behold her, their glorious Queen.

Mary's Unlimited Power

Of all creatures Mary, as the Mother of God, possesses the highest power in heaven. She prays, but not as the saints do. In a way she has unlimited power in her prayers because Jesus will not resist the motherly authority He Himself gave her. How can He, who has assumed flesh of her flesh, resist her appeal? She uses this wonderful power for the benefit of her children, especially those who tenderly love her and venerate her as their Mother.

We should pray to the Queen of All Saints for the grace to remember that God has created us to live a life of holiness in this world and to become saints in heaven. God will give us enough grace to do this if only we have an earnest desire for holiness just as Mary did. Holiness does not consist in heroic deeds, but in doing the will of God perfectly, loving God with all our heart and our neighbor for God's sake, keeping our soul from sin, and being united with God through prayer and the sacraments. We should pray to Mary to obtain for us the grace to imitate her holiness in this world and enjoy the vision of God and her presence for all eternity in heaven.

As Mediatrix with Jesus, Mary shares also in His supreme authority over the universe. She is Queen because she is the Mother of the Word Incarnate. Christ is universal King because He rules all creatures by His personal union with the Divinity. It was God's plan for Mary to bring Him into the world that He might be King, according to the words of the archangel, "His reign will be without end."

Mary is Queen also because she is co-redemptrix. Jesus reigns over us not only by natural right, but also by the right of redemption. As cooperator with her Son in that work of redemption, Mary also acquired the right to reign with Him. God chose her to be His Mother and by that very choice has associated her with Himself in the work of the salvation of mankind.

Our Spiritual Mother

Mary's is the queenship of goodness. She adds a degree of motherly sweetness to the joy of the angels and saints and to be blessed of the Church triumphant. To the Church suffering she brings consolation, relief, deliverance; to the Church militant she offers aid, confidence, victory.

Mary's place in the Church is second only to Christ because she is the ever-virgin Mother of Jesus Christ our Lord and God, and because she is very close to us as our spiritual Mother and our Queen. We owe special veneration by word and example to Mary as Mother of Christ, Mother of the Church, and our spiritual Mother and Queen. By following her example and by seeking her help in prayer we can be sure of reaching her Son in eternal life.

The feast of the Queenship of Mary is celebrated on August 22, on which day the Church prays: "O God, You have given us the Mother of Your Son to be our Mother and Queen. Through her intercession, grant that we may attain the glory destined for Your adopted sons in Your heavenly Kingdom."

JOSEPH

JOSEPH was privileged to share in the mystery of the Incarnation as the foster-father of Jesus. Mary alone was directly connected with the fulfillment of the mystery when she gave her consent to Christ's conception and allowed the Holy Spirit to form the sacred humanity of Jesus from her blood. Joseph had a part in this mystery in an indirect way when he fulfilled the condition necessary for the Incarnation, that is, the protection of Mary's virginity before and during his married life with her. He made the virginal marriage possible, and this was a part of God's plan from all eternity.

Joseph's Role as Foster-Father

In a more direct manner Joseph shared in the support, upbringing, and protection of the Divine Child as His foster-father. For this purpose he was given the true heart of a father—a heart full of love and self-sacrifice. Through the toil of his hands he was able to offer protection to the Divine Child, providing for Him food, clothing, and a home. He was truly the saint of the holy childhood of Jesus—the living created providence which watched over the Christ-Child.

When Herod sought the Child to put Him to death, the Heavenly Father sent an angelic messenger, giving orders for the flight; the rest He left entirely in Joseph's hands. It was Joseph's fatherly love that was then the only refuge which received and protected the Divine Child. His fatherly love carried Him through the desert into Egypt till all enemies were removed. Then, under his safekeeping, the Child returned to Nazareth to be nourished and provided for by the labor of his hands for many years. Whatever a human son owes to a human father for all the benefits of his upbringing and support, Jesus owed to Joseph, because Joseph was to Him a foster-father, teacher, and protector.

Joseph served the Divine Child with a singular love. God gave him a heart filled with heavenly, supernatural love—a love far deeper and more powerful than any natural father's love could be.

Joseph served the Divine Child with great unselfishness, without any regard to self-interest, but not without sacrifices. He did not toil for himself, but he seemed to be an instrument intended for the benefit of others, to be put aside as soon as it had done its work, for Scripture no longer mentions him once the childhood of Jesus had passed.

Joseph was the shadow of the Heavenly Father not only as His earthly representative, but also by appearing to be Christ's natural father, he was able to hide for a while the divinity of Jesus.

Joseph's Role as Husband

Joseph is also the true husband of Mary. Scripture says: "Jacob was the father of Joseph the husband of Mary. It was of her that Jesus who is called the Messiah was born" (Mt 1:16). His marriage to Mary was a sacred contract by which he and Mary gave themselves to each other. Mary really belonged to him with all she was and had. He had a right to her love and obedience; and no other person so won her esteem, obedience, and love.

Joseph was also the protector and witness of Mary's virginity. In their marriage he and Mary gave to each other their virginity, and also the mutual right over it— a right to safeguard the other's virtue. This mutual virginity also belonged in the divine plan of the Incarnation, for God sent His angel to assure Joseph that Mary's motherhood and virginity could be united.

This marital union not only brought Joseph into daily association with Mary, the loveliest of God's creatures, but also enabled him to behold continually all her virtues and to share with her a mutual exchange of spiritual goods. And Mary found spiritual enlightenment in Joseph's calm, humble, and deep virtue, purity, and sanctity. A great honor came to Joseph from this union with her whom the Son of God called Mother and whom He declared the Queen of heaven and earth.

God the Son confided the guardianship and the support of His immaculate Mother to Joseph's care. Mary's life was that of the Mother of the Savior, who did not come upon earth to enjoy honors and pleasures, but to redeem the world by hard work, suffering, and the Cross. Joseph was the faithful companion, support, and comforter of the Mother of Sorrows. He was loyal to her in poverty, journeying, work, and pain. His love for Mary was based upon His esteem for her as Mother of God. After God and the Divine Child, he loved no one as much as he loved her. Mary responded to this love. She submitted to Joseph's guidance with naturalness and easy grace and childlike confidence. The Holy Spirit himself was the bond of the great love which united their hearts.

Joseph lived for one purpose—to be the personal servant of Jesus Christ, the Word made flesh. His simple birth which traces his line from noble ancestry of Abraham and King David, the graces and gifts, so generously poured out on him by God—all this was his to serve the Lord better. Every thought, word, and action of his was a homage to the love and glory of the Incarnate Word. He fulfilled most faithfully the role of a good and faithful servant who cared for the House of God.

Joseph, the Patron of Family Life

God has made Joseph a heavenly patron not only of the Catholic Church but also of family life because he sanctified himself as head of the Holy Family. By this beautiful example, he sanctified family life. How peacefully and happily the Holy Family rested under the care of his fatherly rule, even in the midst of trials. He was the protector, counselor, and consolation of the Holy Family in every need. Just as Joseph was the model of piety, so he gave us by his zeal, earnestness, devout trust in God's providence, and especially by his love, the example of labor according to the Will of God. He cherished all the experiences common to family life and the sacred memories of the shared life, sufferings, and joys with Jesus and Mary. In his loving fatherliness and unfailing intercession, Joseph is the patron and protector of families, and he deserves a place in every home.

Joseph worked at Nazareth as a carpenter. It was the Will of God that he and his foster-Son spend their days together in manual labor. They set a beautiful example for the working population.

It was fitting that at the hour of Joseph's death Jesus should stand at his bedside with Mary, the sweetness and hope of all mankind. He gave his entire life to the service of Jesus and Mary; at death he enjoyed the consolation of dying in their loving arms.

The feast of Saint Joseph is March 19, on which day the Church prays: "Almighty God, You entrusted to the faithful care of Joseph the beginnings of the mysteries of man's salvation. Through his intercession may Your Church always be faithful in its service so that Your designs will be fulfilled."

JOACHIM AND ANNE

A LL our information concerning Saints Joachim and Anne, the parents of Mary, is derived from a non-canonical Infancy Gospel known as the "Proto-evangelium" of James, which goes back to about A.D. 150.

In Nazareth there lived a devout couple, Joachim and Anne. They were childless, a condition that was held as a bitter misfortune among the Jews. One feast day, Joachim went to the Temple to offer sacrifice, but was turned away by a certain Ruben, who said that men without children were unworthy to be admitted. Grief-stricken, Joachim did not return home, but went into the mountains to plead with God in solitude. Also Anne, having learned the reason for the prolonged absence of her husband, cried to the Lord to take away from her the curse of sterility, and she promised to dedicate her child to the service of God.

Their prayers were heard. An angel came to Joachim and Anne and promised them a daughter. They named their daughter Miriam or Mary and offered the child to God in the service of the Temple at a very early age.

The Grandparents of Jesus

Anne is the grandmother of Jesus. This title is the foundation of all the other privileges which surround her with glory. God had decided that the world was to be restored to the life of grace by the Word of God made Man. From all eternity Anne's daughter had been chosen as the Mother of this Redeemer. Her blood flowed in Mary's veins, and hence also in those of Jesus. Now, by grace, we are the brothers and sisters of Jesus who is Anne's Grandson by nature; so we are, as it were, her grandchildren for we all belong to the family of God.

God the Father loves Anne as the mother of His beloved daughter Mary. God the Son loves her for having given Him a Mother through whom He became Man and the Savior of the world. God the Holy Spirit loves her for having given Him so beautiful and worthy a spouse. The angels and the saints in heaven honor her as the Mother of their Queen. The just and sinners turn to her as to their powerful advocate before God, and by her intercession they hope for grace and forgiveness.

Anne was privileged to satisfy the earliest wants of Mary and to watch over her infancy. Together with the Holy Spirit, she worked in educating Mary to prepare her for the highest vocation ever given to a woman—to be the Mother of God's own Son. She presented her to the Lord in the Temple and consecrated her to the service of God. She rejoiced at Mary's share in the Redemption as the mother of the Divine Redeemer. And when, after her daughter's glorious Assumption into heaven, she crossed the heavenly courts to accept her own heavenly glory, Anne received from the angels and saints the honors due to her as the mother of Mary. And now she enjoys for all eternity—together with her husband Joachim—the tender love and unsurpassed glory of her loving daughter Mary and the love of her Grandson Jesus.

Patroness of Christian Families

St. Anne is the patroness and support of Christian families. She was deeply devoted to her husband, Joachim, with holy, chaste, and constant love. With zealous care she watched over and trained her little daughter, Mary, that she might become the Mother of God's Son. As guardian of the infancy and childhood of the Virgin Mary, she showed the sanctity and dignity of work as an expression of God's will and the need of religion as the foundation for happy family life. Through her intercession she can obtain for all who enter the married state the graces they need, that imitating her virtues, they may sanctify their homes and lead the souls entrusted to their care to eternal glory.

The feast of Saints Joachim and Anne is July 26, on which day the Church prays: "Lord, God of our fathers, through Saints Joachim and Anne You gave us the Mother of Your Incarnate Son. May their prayers help us to attain the salvation You promised to Your people."

PAUL OF TARSUS

JESUS Christ announced the Gospel, but the Church was not merely to repeat what He said. Christianity proclaimed Jesus as its content, and Paul was foremost in establishing that message as a universal religion. He was the most important personality in the first generation of Christians.

Paul was born in the beginning of the first century A.D. in Tarsus, a Greek-Roman city on the southern coast of what is now Turkey. His father may have been wealthy, since Paul was a Roman citizen, a privileged status often inherited. His primary language was Greek, though he was raised in strict Jewish belief and practice. Since he intended to be a rabbi, he learned a trade, as was customary for young students. He supported himself on his preaching tours as a tent maker or leather worker.

Paul went to Jerusalem at a young age to study the Jewish law "at the feet of Gamaliel," as he says (Acts 22:3). Rabbi Gamaliel was a famous teacher.

Although Jesus of Nazareth and Paul of Tarsus were born about the same time, they never met while Jesus was on earth. Paul encountered the risen Lord Jesus Christ around A.D. 35 in a moving revelation on the road from Jerusalem to Damascus. He considered this experience as his call to an apostleship as valid as that of any who had walked with Jesus.

Paul's Persecution of the Church

Before his conversion he was known as Saul, which was his Jewish name. The Acts of the Apostles has a striking description of that conversion. Paul also describes it in his letters. Saul opposed the new Church. The Book of Acts reports him as present and consenting to the stoning of Stephen, the first Christian martyr. It is not clear whether he persecuted the Church officially or whether he was personally motivated. Paul in his Letter to the Galatians simply says he "made progress in Jewish observance far beyond most of my contemporaries, in excess of zeal to live out all the traditions of my ancestors" (1:14). He says he "went to extremes in persecuting the church of God and tried to destroy it" (1:13).

Acts says that Saul, still breathing murderous threats against the Lord's disciples, went to the high priest and asked him for letters to the synagogues in Damascus which would empower him to arrest and bring to Jerusalem anyone he might find, man or woman, living according to the new way.

Saul's Conversion

As he traveled along and was approaching Damascus, a light from the sky suddenly flashed about him. He fell to the ground and at the same time heard a voice saying: "Saul, Saul, why do you persecute me?"

"Who are You, sir? he asked.

The voice answered: "I am Jesus, the One you are persecuting. Get up and go into the city, where you will be told what to do."

The men who were traveling with him stood there speechless. They had heard the voice but could see no one. Saul got up from the ground unable to see, even though his eyes were open. They had to take him by the hand and lead him into Damascus. For three days he continued blind during which time he neither ate nor drank.

There was a disciple in Damascus named Ananias to whom the Lord had appeared in a vision. "Ananias!" He said.

"Here I am, Lord," came the answer.

The Lord said to him, "Go at once to Straight Street, and at the house of Judas ask for a certain Saul of Tarsus. He is there praying." (Saul saw in a vision a man named Ananias coming to him and placing his hands on him so that he might recover his sight.)

But Ananias protested: "Lord, I have heard from many sources about this man and all the harm he has done to Your holy people in Jerusalem. He is here now with authorization from the chief priests to arrest any who invoke Your name."

The Lord said to him: "You must go! This name is the instrument I have chosen to bring My name to the Gentiles and their kings and to the people of Israel. I Myself shall indicate to him how much he will have to suffer for My word."

With that Ananias left. When he entered the house he laid his hands on Saul and said: "Saul, my brother, I have been sent by the Lord Jesus who appeared to you on the way here, to help you recover your sight and be filled with the Holy Spirit." Immediately something like scales fell from his eyes and he regained his sight. He got up and was baptized, and his strength returned to him after he had taken food.

Saul stayed some time with the disciples in Damascus, and soon he began to proclaim in the synagogues that Jesus was the Son of God. Saul for his part grew steadily more powerful and reduced the Jewish community of Damascus to silence with his proofs that this Jesus was the Messiah.

After quite some time had passed, certain Jews conspired to kill Saul, but their plot came to his attention.

Some of his disciples, therefore, took him along the wall one night and lowered him to the ground, using ropes and a hamper. When he arrived back in Jerusalem he tried to join the disciples there. Then Barnabas took him in charge and introduced him to the apostles. He explained to them how on his journey Saul had seen the Lord, who had conversed with him. Saul stayed on with them, moving freely about Jerusalem and expressing himself quite openly in the name of the Lord. But Jerusalem was not his base of operations after he became a missionary.

Paul had been the most Pharisaic of Pharisees, the most legalistic of Mosaic lawyers, Now he suddenly appeared to his fellow Jews as a heretical welcomer of Gentiles, a traitor and apostate.

Paul's central conviction was that only God can save human beings. Nothing we can do, even the most strict observance of the Law, is enough to bring to God as reparation for sin or as payment for grace. To be saved from ourselves, from sin, from the devil, and from death, we must open ourselves completely to the saving power of Jesus.

Paul's Missionary Work

Although Paul carried on a lifelong debate with his fellow Jews about the uselessness of the Law without Christ, he never lost his love for them. He reminded the Gentiles that they were grafted on the parent stock of the Jews, who were still God's chosen people, the children of the promise. Paul was the instrument Christ used to save Christianity from slavery to the Law as a means of salvation and to enrich the newly engrafted Gentile branches with the precious heritage of the Jews.

It is clear that Damascus, and later Antioch, were Paul's early headquarters. He did not consider himself under the jurisdiction of the Jerusalem Church. He did not request a commission for his missionary journeys, the first taking him to Cyprus and cities of Asia Minor, the second extending his work into Greece, and the third a long swing revisiting many churches established in both Asia and Europe.

Paul was the first to realize the contrast between the Gospel of Christ and the Jewish world from which it came, and also the first to understand that the Church could not be ethnically restricted. A Jew who never rejected his Jewish heritage, Paul was the Apostle to the Gentiles.

According to Paul, correct relation to God is based entirely on the initiative of God, the giver of law and of grace in Jesus Christ. Law and human failure to keep it, he said, shows the depth of human pride and sin. But grace in Jesus Christ vanquishes sin and establishes peace between God and humanity. He presented Christ as the "new Adam" replacing the old, fallen one from whose nature persons are saved by God's gifts of faith and obedience. That, to Paul, is righteousness.

Tension over the mixture of Jews and Gentiles in the Church became so intense that all the major leaders gathered in Jerusalem to consider the issue. Peter made the primary speech against imposing Jewish law on Gentile believers. Paul and his colleage Barnabas were present and spoke. James proposed a compromise: Gentiles should not trouble themselves with Jewish observances, except that they should abstain from meat sacrificed to pagan idols, from pagan worship involving sex, and from eating anything containing blood, a practice prohibited to Jews.

To Paul, Jesus Christ is the Gospel, the living revelation of God's goodness, love, and grace—righteousness to those of faith. In Christ, he taught, God is making right the relationship not only between God and people but also among people. Paul worked eagerly that Jews and Gentiles alike might hear and believe this Good News. Faith, not the letter of the Law, he said, is what matters.

His experiencing the personal risen Jesus on the road to Damascus was the driving force that made Paul one of the most zealous, dynamic, and courageous ambassadors of Christ the Church has ever had. But persecution, humiliation, and weakness became his daily cross. The dying Christ was in him; the living Christ was his life.

Paul's Suffering

By Paul's own admission he had an ailment or deformity that pained him. He called it his "thorn in the flesh." In addition to this, Paul experienced suffering and deprivation in the course of his missionary trips. His own words summarize it best:

"Five times at the hands of the Jews I received forty lashes less one; three times I was beaten with rods; I was stoned once, shipwrecked three times; I passed a day and a night on the sea. I traveled continually, endangered by floods, robbers, my own people, the Gentiles; imperiled in the city, in the desert, at sea, by false brothers; enduring labor, hardship, many sleepless nights; in hunger and thirst and frequent fastings, in cold and nakedness. Leaving other sufferings unmentioned, there is that daily tension pressing on me, my anxiety for all churches" (2 Cor 11:24-28).

"But I refrain, lest anyone think more of me than what he sees in me or hears from my lips. As to the extraordinary revelations, in order that I might not become conceited I was given a thorn in the flesh, an angel of Satan to beat me and keep me from getting proud. Three times I begged the Lord that this might leave me. He said to me, 'My grace is enough for you, for in weakness power reaches perfection.' And so I willingly boast of my weaknesses instead, that the power of Christ may rest upon me. Therefore I am content with weakness, with mistreatment, with distress, with persecutions and difficulties for the sake of Christ; for when I am powerless, it is then that I am strong" (2 Cor 12:7-10).

Anxiety over the churches he had founded or nurtured was one motivation for most of the letters of Paul found in the New Testament. They were often written in response to questions or to resolve controversies in the young congregations. His most systematic statement of faith is found in the Letter to the Romans, a letter of self-introduction to a church he did not found. He kept meaning to go to Rome—he did, finally, in chains.

Paul went to Jerusalem to deliver a contribution made by the Gentile congregations. He was attacked in the Temple by Jews aroused by reports that he had taken Greeks into the inner court, something forbidden to non-Jews. Rescued by Roman soldiers who learned he was a Roman citizen, Paul was held in protective custody, and later transferred to Caesarea when a plot against him was discovered. He had two choices as a Roman citizen: either have the Jewish charges against him heard by the Roman governor in Jerusalem, or appeal to Caesar in Rome. He chose to go to Rome.

Shipwrecked off Malta, he was transferred to another boat, which reached Italy. Paul lived in Rome, restricted but not confined, awaiting his hearing before the Roman ruler, probably Nero. He wrote some of his most important letters in Rome. The Acts of the Apostles ends with him there: "For two years Paul lived there in a place he rented for himself, and welcomed all who came to see him. He preached about the Kingdom of God and taught about the Lord Jesus Christ, speaking with all boldness and freedom" (Acts 28:30-31).

It is said that Nero finally dismissed the charges and Paul resumed his career, perhaps going to preach in Spain. He was seized a second time and executed by Nero about A.D. 65. Tradition says that he was beheaded.

Paul took the Christian faith into the Roman world, gave the Church its enduring theological direction, and forced succeeding generations to look for truth in the Cross of Jesus Christ. He wrote: "For God's folly is wiser than men, and his weakness more powerful than men" (1 Cor 1:25).

Paul speaks of this wisdom in these words: "I have come to rate all as loss in the light of the surpassing knowledge of my Lord Jesus Christ. For His sake I have forfeited everything; I have accounted all else rubbish so that Christ may be my wealth and I may be in Him, not having any justice of my own based on observance of the Law. The justice I possess is that which comes through faith in Christ. It has its origin in God and is based on faith. I wish to know Christ and the power flowing from His resurrection; likewise to know how to share in His sufferings by being formed into the pattern of His death. Thus do I hope that I may arrive at resurrection from the dead. It is not that I have reached it yet, or have already finished my course; but I am racing to grasp the prize if possible, since I have been grasped by Christ (Jesus). Brothers, I do not think of myself as having reached the finish line. I give no thought to what lies behind but push on to what is ahead. My entire attention is on the finish line as I run toward the prize to which God calls me—life on high in Christ Jesus" (Phil 3:8-14).

The feast of Saint Peter and Saint Paul is June 29. The Church prays: "O God, by the preaching of Saint Paul, the Apostle, You taught the multitudes of the Gentiles. Grant that we who venerate his example may also share in his prayers."

STEPHEN, FIRST MARTYR
(d. 36)

ALL we know of Stephen is found in chapters 6 and 7 of the Acts of the Apostles. The Apostles told the disciples to choose seven men who lived a holy life to help in the care of the poor. These men were called deacons, and Stephen was named first of the deacons who served the Jerusalem Church. The Apostles ordained them deacons by praying and placing their hands upon them.

Stephen "was a man filled with grace and power, who worked great wonders and signs among the people. Certain members of the so-called 'Synagogue of Roman Freedmen' (that is, the Jews from Cyrene, Alexandria,

Cicilia and Asia) would undertake to engage Stephen in debate, but they proved no match for the wisdom and spirit with which he spoke. They persuaded some men to make the charge that they had heard him speaking blasphemies against Moses and God, and in this way they incited the people, the elders, and the scribes. All together they confronted him, seized him, and led him off to the Sanhedrin. There they brought in false witnesses. . . . The members of the Sanhedrin who sat there stared at him intently. Throughout, Stephen's face seemed like that of an angel."

Stephen's Martydom

The Acts of the Apostles describes his martyrdom. "Those who listened to his words were stung to the heart; they ground their teeth in anger at him. Stephen meanwhile, filled with the Holy Spirit, looked to the sky above and saw the glory of God and Jesus standing at God's right hand. 'Look!' he exclaimed, 'I see an opening in the sky, and the Son of Man standing at God's right hand.'

"The onlookers were shouting aloud, holding their hands over their ears as they did so. Then they rushed at him as one man, dragged him out of the city, and began to stone him. The witnesses meanwhile were piling their cloaks at the feet of a young man named Saul. As Stephen was being stoned he could be heard praying, 'Lord Jesus, receive my spirit.' He fell to his knees and cried out in a loud voice, 'Lord, do not hold this sin against them.' And with that he died. Saul, for his part, concurred in the act of killing" (Acts 6:8—8:1).

Stephen died as Jesus did: falsely accused, brought to unjust condemnation because he spoke the truth fearlessly. He died with his eyes trustfully fixed on Christ and with a prayer of forgiveness on his lips.

Stephen was the first martyr. His feast is celebrated on December 26, on which the Church prays: "O God, grant that we may imitate the saint we honor and love our enemies. For today we celebrate the feast of Saint Stephen who knew how to pray even for his persecutors."

CECILIA
(d. 117)

T HE most celebrated account of the life of Cecilia is contained in the "Acts" of her martyrdom, written in the fifth century. Probably only the main facts of this document are from authentic sources.

Cecilia was born in Rome. Although her father was a pagan, she probably had a Christian mother. She belonged to a noble patrician family, whose ancestors were widely known and esteemed in Roman history.

Cecilia was very rich and distinguished, but she lived a life of prayer and penance. When she was very young, her father gave her in marriage to a youthful pagan patrician named Valerian. On the wedding day,

31

amid the music and rejoicing of the guests, she sat apart, singing to God in her heart. She renewed the vow by which she had consecrated her virginity to God.

Cecilia converted her husband to the faith of Christ. Because he helped Cecilia in her charity toward the poor, he was put to death. Later Cecilia was arrested. She chose death rather than sacrifice to the gods and renounce her faith.

Cecilia's Death

Fearing that her youth, her nobility, and above all her charity to the poor would arouse the people if she were executed publicly, Almachius, the Prefect of Rome, had her imprisoned in the vapor or steam bath of her own home that she might die of suffocation. Around the walls of this room ran leaden pipes which were heated to such a high degree that death seemed inevitable.

Cecilia remained a whole day and night in this stifling steam without suffering any harm. Finding himself forced to shed the blood of this Roman lady, Almachius sent an executioner to behead her. With trembling hand he struck the three blows which the law allowed but failed to cut off the head of Cecilia. She fell to the floor. For two days and nights she lay on the pavement of her bath, alive and fully conscious, with her head half-severed.

The Christians rushed in after the hasty departure of the executioner and, with linen cloths, wiped up the blood flowing from her wounds, but did not raise her from the floor. On the third morning the venerable Bishop Urban came to say good-bye to Cecilia. As she lay dying, she requested that her palace be made into a church and that the poor she had always loved should be cared for. She was lying on her right side, her hands as if crossed in prayer before her. She turned her face to the floor so that no one might disturb her last secret communing with God and then expired. A story relates that the position of her fingers—three extended on her right hand and one on the left—were her final silent profession of faith in the Holy Trinity. Her death probably occurred in the year 177.

The Christians laid Cecilia, clothed in the rich robe of silk and gold she had worn at the time of her martyrdom, in a cypress coffin in the same position in which she had expired. At her feet they placed the linen cloth and veils with which the faithful had collected her blood. The following night they carried her body out to the Appian Way and buried her in the crypt of the Cecilii, near the crypt of the Popes, in the Catacomb of Saint Callistus.

Cecilia Appears In a Vision

In 817 Pope Paschal I transferred to different churches in the city the relics of 2,300 martyrs from the various catacombs. The catacombs at that time were lying in a deplorable state of ruin. He could not find the tomb of Saint Cecilia. It is alleged that four years later she appeared to him in a vision and told him where her body lay. He discovered the tomb of Cecilia. She reposed in her cypress coffin. Her body was fresh and perfect as when it was first laid in the tomb. On May 8, 822, the Pontiff solemnly dedicated the Church of Santa Cecilia in Trastevere and put her relics into the crypt of the church.

When her tomb was opened in 1599, her body was perfectly incorrupt and entire. The saint was lying on her right side. The neck still bore marks of the sword, and the head was turned toward the bottom of the coffin. The body lay exposed for veneration for five weeks.

Cardinal Sfondrati erected the beautiful high altar which now stands over the saint's tomb. He summoned Stefano Maderna, the most skillful sculptor of his day, to make an exact reproduction of the figure in marble. The sculptor engraved this testimony on the case: "Behold the most holy virgin Cecilia, whom I myself saw lying incorrupt in her tomb. I have made for you in this marble an image of that saint in the very posture of her body." This statue is in the church of St. Cecilia, under the altar close to the place where the relics were reburied.

St. Cecilia is often glorified in poetry and music. She is one of the most venerated martyrs of Christian antiquity. She is regarded as the patroness of church music because of the zeal with which she sang the divine praises.

During the years of bloody persecution which followed the martyrdom of Saint Cecilia, the example of this young and beautiful maiden who, in the worldly sense, had everything to live for, inspired thousands of Christians with generous devotion to Christ and His Church. But, most of all, she is a brilliant model of purity, because she dedicated the purity of her body and soul to Christ and declared before her persecutors: "I am the bride of my Lord Jesus Christ."

The feast of Saint Cecilia is November 22, on which the Church prays: "O Lord, hear our requests. Through the intercession of Cecilia, please grant what we ask."

AGNES
(d. 258)

LEGEND has it that Agnes was a beautiful girl whom many young men wanted to marry. Among those she refused, one reported her to the authorities as being a Christian. She was arrested and confined to a house of prostitution.

She was led to the altar of the pagan goddess Minerva in Rome to offer incense to her. But she raised her hands to Jesus Christ and made the Sign of the Cross.

The soldiers bound her hands and feet. Her young hands were so thin that the chains slipped from her wrists for she was only twelve years old. When the judge saw that she was not afraid of pain, he had her clothes stripped off, and she had to stand in the street before a pagan crowd. She cried out: "Christ will guard His own." A story relates that the one who looked upon her lustfully lost his sight and had it restored by her prayer.

Agnes Is Executed

After having prayed, she bowed her neck to the sword. At one stroke her head was cut off, and the angels took her soul to heaven. This happened about the year 258.

In the Divine Office she is quoted as saying: "Christ is my Spouse. He chose me first and His I will be. He made my soul beautiful with the jewels of grace and virtue. I belong to Him whom the angels serve."

The name Agnes comes from the Latin word "agnus," meaning lamb, and reminds us of the gentleness of this young saint.

Pope Damasus adorned her tomb with sacred poetry, and many of the Fathers of the Church, following Saint Ambrose, have honored her in their writings. Saint Ambrose speaks of Agnes in his *Treatise on Virgins:* "Today is the birthday of a virgin; let us imitate her integrity. It is the birthday of a martyr; let us offer sacrifices. It is the birthday of Saint Agnes, who is said to have suffered martyrdom at the age of twelve. The more abominable was the cruelty that did not spare that young age, the greater was the power of faith that received the witness even of such youth. . . .

"This is a new kind of martyrdom! She is not fit for punishment but already ripe for victory. It is difficult for her to do battle but easy to be crowned. Although she bore the disadvantage of youth, she achieved a masterpiece of valor. A bride would not have started out toward her bridal bed with so much solicitude as this virgin gladly hurried to the place of torture, her head adorned not with braids but with Christ and crowned not with flowers but with virtue. . . . In a single victim we have a double martyrdom: of restraint and of faith. She remained a virgin and became a martyr.

"This is a virgin's birthday; let us follow the example of her chastity. Let human beings be filled with wonder, little ones with hope, married women with awe, and the unmarried with emulation. It seems to me that this child, holy beyond her years and courageous beyond human nature, received the name of Agnes, meaning pure in Greek, not as an earthly designation but as a revelation from God of what she was to be."

Symbol of Holiness

Agnes is a symbol that holiness does not depend on length of years, experience or human effort. It is a gift God offers to all, one He can protect in the most fearful of circumstances.

The feast day of Saint Agnes is January 21, on which the Church prays: "All-powerful and ever-living God, You choose the weak in this world to confound the powerful. As we celebrate the anniversary of the martyrdom of Saint Agnes, may we like her remain constant in faith."

LAWRENCE
(d. 258)

L AWRENCE was the first of the seven deacons who served the Church at Rome. His duty was to assist the Pope when celebrating Holy Mass and to give Holy Communion to the people. He was also in charge of the Church property, distributing among the poor the offerings given by the Christians.

When Pope St. Sixtus II was led out to die, Lawrence wept that he, too, could not die along with him. The Pope said: "Do not cry, my son; in three days you will follow me."

When Lawrence knew he would be arrested like the Pope, he sought out the poor, widows, and orphans of

Rome and gave them all the money he had on hand, selling even the sacred vessels to increase the sum. When the prefect of Rome heard of this, he imagined that the Christians must have considerable treasure. He sent for Lawrence and said: "You Christians say we are cruel to you, but that is not what I have in mind. I am told that your priests offer in gold, that the sacred blood is received in silver cups, that you have golden candlesticks at your evening services. Now, your doctrine says you must render to Caesar what is his. Bring these treasures—the emperor needs them to maintain his forces."

Lawrence Offers the Treasures of the Church

Lawrence replied that the Church was indeed rich. "I will show you a valuable part. But give me time to set everything in order and make an inventory." After three days he gathered a great number of the blind, lame, maimed, lepers, orphans, and widows and put them in rows. When the prefect arrived, Lawrence simply said: "These are the treasures of the Church."

The prefect was so angry he told Lawrence that he would indeed have his wish to die. He had a great griddle prepared, with coals beneath it, and had Lawrence's body placed on it. Legend has it that after the martyr had suffered the pain for a long time, he made his famous cheerful remark: "My body is well done. Turn it over; it is roasted enough on that side." Lawrence died in 258.

Lawrence is one of those whose martyrdom made a deep and lasting impression on the early Church. Celebration of his feastday spread rapidly. Legendary details of his death were known to Damasus, Prudentius, Ambrose, and Augustine. Saint Augustine writes: "The

Church of Rome invites us today to celebrate the day when Saint Lawrence triumphed. On this day he brought down the fury of the world and rejected its allurement— thus twice vanquishing the persecuting demon.

"As you know, Lawrence held the office of deacon in the Church of Rome. In that office he administered the sacred blood of Christ to the faithful and in that office he also shed his own blood for the sake of Christ. Saint John the Apostle clearly highlighted the mystery of the Lord's Supper when he said: 'Just as Jesus laid down His life for us, so must we also lay down our lives for our brothers and sisters.' . . . Lawrence understood this fact and acted in accord with it. What he had received at this table he willed to hold especially dear. He loved Christ by his life and he loved Him by his death as well."

Lawrence's Sacrifice

Little is known about Lawrence, and yet he has received extraordinary honor in the Church since the fourth century. The greatest fact of his life is certain: he died for Christ. We who are hungry for details about the lives of the saints are again reminded that their holiness was, after all, total response to Christ, expressed perfectly by a death like his.

The church built over his tomb became one of the seven principal churches in Rome and a favorite place for Roman pilgrimages.

The feast day of Saint Lawrence is August 10, on which the Church prays: "O God, by his ardent love for You Saint Lawrence exhibited faithful service and attained a glorious martyrdom. Help us to love what he loved and to practice what he taught."

JEROME
(345-420)

JEROME was born at Stridon in Dalmatia now Yugoslavia, in 345. He was sent to school at Rome. He then visited foreign cities, devoted himself to the sciences and oratory, and finally became a lawyer. For a time he lived a worldly life, but later he received baptism at Rome.

He embraced a life of asceticism and went to the East. At Antioch he was ordained a priest. Returning to Rome, he became a secretary to Pope Damasus. At Rome he began to translate the Holy Scriptures into Latin and to promote the monastic life. Eventually he settled in Palestine, where he traveled extensively, marking each spot of Christ's life with an outpouring of his devotion. Mystic that he was, he spent five years in the desert of Chalcis so that he might give himself up to prayer, penance, and study. Finally he settled in Bethlehem where he lived in a cave and served the needs of the Church.

Jerome was above all a Scripture scholar, translating the Old Testament from the Hebrew and the New Testament from the Greek. He also wrote commentaries which are a great source of scriptural inspiration for us today.

The Importance of Scripture

In his commentary on Isaiah, Jerome writes: "I obey the commands of Christ who says: 'Search the Scriptures,' and 'Seek and you shall find.' I do not want Him to say to me what He told the Jews: 'You err because you know neither the Scriptures nor the power of God.' If, as the Apostle Paul states, Christ is the power of God and the wisdom of God, then the person who does not know the Scriptures does not know the power of God and His wisdom: Ignorance of the Scriptures is ignorance of Christ.

"Therefore I will imitate the father of a family who brings forth things both new and old from his storehouse and the bride in the Song of Songs who says: 'I have kept for you, my beloved, fruits both new and old.' I intend to explain Isaiah not only as a Prophet but also as an Evangelist and an Apostle."

Jerome is particularly important for having made a translation of the Bible which came to be called the Vulgate. The Council of Trent called for a new and corrected edition of the Vulgate and declared it to be the authentic text to be used in the Church.

Jerome is said to have had a bad temper, but his love for God and his Son Jesus Christ was extraordinarily intense; anyone who taught error was an enemy of God and truth, and Jerome went after him with his mighty pen. He was a strong, outspoken man, a fearless critic. Yet he was swift to remorse, even more severe on his own shortcomings than on those of others.

Jerome's Temptations

Jerome wrote to St. Eustochium: "In the remotest part of a wild and stony desert, burnt up with the heat of the scorching sun so that it frightens even the monks that inhabit it, I seemed to myself to be in the midst of the delights and crowds of Rome. In this exile and prison to which for the fear of hell I had voluntarily condemned myself, I many times imagined myself witnessing the dancing of the Roman maidens as if I had been in the midst of them; in my cold body and in my parched-up flesh, which seemed dead before its death, passion was able to live. Alone with this enemy, I threw myself in spirit at the feet of Jesus, watering them with my tears, and I tamed my flesh by fasting whole weeks. I am not ashamed to disclose my temptations, but I grieve that I am not now what I then was."

When Jerome died in the year 420, his body was buried at Bethlehem and later removed to Rome. His feast day is celebrated on September 30, on which the Church prays: "O God, You gave Saint Jerome a great love for Holy Scripture. Let Your people feed more abundantly on Your word and find in it the source of life."

AUGUSTINE OF HIPPO
(354-430)

A UGUSTINE was born in the North African village of Tagaste (now Souk-Ahras, Algeria), in 354. His mother Monica was a devout, uneducated Christian; his father Patricius, a poor Roman freeman, remained unbaptized until shortly before his death in 371. Augustine, like his brother and sister, was instructed in Monica's faith as a child; baptism was delayed, a common practice in the late fourth century.

Augustine had little interest in the Church. Monica cried and prayed for the conversion of husband and son but avoided nagging. At age eleven the boy was sent to school at Madaura. After Madaura he went to Carthage where he perfected his taste for fleshly recreation as much as he developed the mind. By eighteen he had a mistress and a son, Adeodatus. His times were truly decadent—politically, socially, morally.

Augustine's Search

Augustine felt an inner longing that his "unholy loves" and his professional ambition did not satisfy. The Christian Scriptures his mother urged him to read bored him. He joined a group called the Manichees. Manichaeism teaches about a war between good and evil, light and darkness. The material world is part of the realm of evil; individual souls are sparks of light trapped in darkness, and God sent Jesus to free the sparks. For nine years Augustine attributed his physical lust and drive for fame to his material self, but he kept his mistress, and therefore could be only a low-level Manichee. "O God, give me chastity, but not yet," he prayed.

His continued spiritual dissatisfaction, the death of a close friend, and unruly students in Carthage, where he had become a teacher, led him to Rome. Here he fell in with a group of skeptics who helped free him from Manichaeism without pointing him to Christ. In 384 he left the city to teach in Milan.

Milan was the home of Bishop Ambrose, a great preacher and foe of the remnant of organized Roman paganism. Augustine went to hear Ambrose's sermons. He began to read the Bible. His body continued to complicate his life. His mistress and son were in Milan with him.

Augustine's Conversion

In the summer of 386 while sitting in a garden he had an experience which he describes in his book called *Confessions*. "I heard from a neighboring house a voice, as of a boy or girl, I know not, chanting, and oft repeating, 'Take up and read; take up and read.' I arose; interpreting it to be no other than a command from God, to open the book and read the first chapter I should find. . . . Eagerly then I returned to the place where I laid the volume of the Apostle. I seized, opened, and in silence read that section on which my eyes first fell: 'Let us live honorably as in daylight; not in carousing and drunkenness, not in sexual excess and lust, not in quarreling and jealousy. Rather, put on the Lord Jesus Christ and make no provision for the desires of the flesh' " (Rom 13:13-14).

Augustine diligently prepared for baptism, performed by Ambrose on Easter, 387. This was a turning point in his life; however, he was not immediately transformed into a theologian. That would come gradually.

After Augustine's baptism in Milan, Monica wanted to return to Tagaste. Her son resolved to go with her, taking Adeodatus, and there establish a retreat house for Christian study and devotion, but at Ostia, the port of Rome, Monica fell sick and died.

In his *Confessions* Augustine speaks of his mother in these words: "The day was near when my mother Monica was to depart from this world, a day known to You, O Lord, but not to us. . . . She and I were standing alone, leaning upon the window that looked out onto the garden of the house where we were staying, at Ostia on the Tiber. . . .

"My mother said to me: 'Son, for my part, there is nothing in this life that gives me any delight. What I have to do here any longer or why I am here I do not know; all my hopes of this world are now at an end. One thing there was for which I did desire to stay a little longer in this life, which was that I might see you a Catholic before I died. And my God has granted me this more abundantly in that I see you now despising all worldly happiness and devoted to His service. What have I now to do here?' . . .

"Scarcely five days or not many more had passed after this before she fell into a fever. . . . My brother and I rushed to her side. . . . She said to us: 'Bury this body anywhere; do not be concerned with that. I ask only one thing: Wherever you may be, remember me at the altar of the Lord.' Once she had put this desire into words for us, she fell silent, for the disease grew worse and gave her great pain."

Augustine Becomes a Priest

Augustine prayed and wrote in relative seclusion for three years. In 391 he was ordained a priest by the bishop of Hippo. Five years later he succeeded Valerius as bishop.

Hippo was a small, unimportant town, but for thirty-four years it was the theological center of the Western Church. It was Augustine who defended Catholic truth against a series of strong heretical movements, including the Manichees. His writings and the doctrinal issues he addressed are too many to enumerate. He wrote against Pelagius, a British monk, who denied original sin. The monk was condemned by the Council of Ephesus in 431.

Augustine's masterpiece was *The City of God*. In the thirteen years of its writing it developed into a theology of history. "The earthly city is determined by self-love, whereas the city of God is constituted by the love of God," he wrote. To Augustine, the Church can be considered the city of God.

Hunger and thirst for righteousness, Augustine taught, is a gift of God setting souls on a quest toward being found in God. God, to him, initiates and finishes with His grace the human pilgrimage toward truth, love, and salvation. He saw his own life as a God-directed pilgrimage from dry ground to the waters of faith and wisdom flowing both to and from God. He understood history as moving to and from the city of God. Augustinian theology provided Europe's religious and social framework for almost a thousand years after the fall of Imperial Rome. Renewal movements in the Church and theology often reach back to Augustine.

A memorable quote from his *Confessions* is one in which he describes his thirst. "Too late have I loved You, O Beauty of ancient days, yet ever new! Too late have I loved You! And behold, You were within, and I abroad, and there I searched for You; I was deformed, plunging amid those fair forms, which You had made. You were with me, but I was not with You. Things held me far from You—things which, if they were not in You. were not at all. You called, and shouted, and burst my deafness. You flashed and shone, and scattered my blindness. You breathed odors and I drew in breath—and I pant for You. I tasted, and I hunger and thirst. You touched me, and I burned for Your peace."

We are all familiar with his prayer: "Our hearts were made for You, O Lord, and they are restless until they rest in You."

His own earthly pilgrimage in grace began in the North African village of Tagaste in 354 and ended seventy-five years later in nearby Hippo, where for thirty-five years he was bishop. His life spanned decades of political upheaval and theological controversy. He died in 430.

The feast day of Saint Augustine is August 28 on which the Church prays: "Lord, renew in Your Church the spirit which You inspired in Saint Augustine, Your bishop. Filled by this spirit, may we thirst after You as the true Source of wisdom."

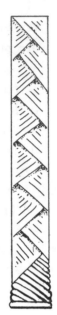

PATRICK
(389-461)

PATRICK was born in England in the year 389. At sixteen he was captured by pirates and sold as a slave to a chief in Ireland. While tending sheep in the mountains, he prayed very frequently and suffered greatly from hunger and cold.

After six years, Patrick escaped and returned to Britain. He later went to Rome, where he became a priest. At the age of 43 he was ordained a bishop. His great desire was to proclaim the Good News to the Irish. The Pope sent him as a missionary to Ireland. Because of the island's pagan background, Patrick was emphatic in encouraging widows to remain chaste and young women to consecrate their virginity to Christ. He ordained many priests, divided the country into dioceses, held Church councils, founded several monasteries, and continually urged his people to greater holiness in Christ. He suffered much opposition from pagan druids.

In a relatively short time the island had deeply experienced the Christian spirit, and it was prepared to send out missionaries whose efforts were greatly responsible for Christianizing Europe.

A Man of Action

Patrick was a man of action, with little inclination toward learning. One of the few authentic writings is his *Confession,* above all an act of homage to God for having called Patrick, unworthy sinner, to the apostolate. In this book he writes:

"I thank God unceasingly because He has kept me faithful in the day of trial. Hence, today I confidently offer my soul as a living sacrifice to Christ my God, who saved me from all distress. And I say to Him: Who am I, O Lord, or to what vocation have You called me, that You have granted me such great heavenly blessings? Thus I constantly exalt and magnify Your Name among the Gentiles wherever I go, and not only in prosperity but also in affliction.

"Therefore, I will accept whatever befalls me, good or bad, and I will ever render thanks to God, who taught me to trust in Him always without hesitation and He will hear me. Not even I know, in these last days, whether I will undertake such a holy and wonderful work, that is, whether I will imitate somehow those who, as the Lord once foretold, would preach His Gospel 'as a witness to all the nations.' . . .

"Should I be worthy, I am ready to give even my life without hesitation and most gladly for His Name, and I desire to spend it thus until I die, if the Lord grants. For I am very much in God's debt. He gave me such grace that through me many peoples were reborn in God and afterward were confirmed, and that clerics were ordained for them everywhere, for a people just coming to the faith, whom the Lord took from the farthest ends of the earth."

The following is a quote from the so-called "Breastplate of Saint Patrick." "May Christ shield me today . . . : Christ with me, Christ before me, Christ behind me. Christ in me, Christ beneath me, Christ above me. Christ on my right, Christ on my left, Christ when I lie down, Christ when I sit, Christ when I stand. Christ in the heart of every person who thinks of me, Christ in the mouth of every person who speaks of me, Christ in every eye that sees me, Christ in every ear that hears me."

Patrick died at Down in 461. His feast day is March 17, on which the Church prays: "O God, You sent Saint Patrick to preach Your glory to the Irish people. Through his merits and intercession grant that we who have the honor of bearing the name of Christians may constantly proclaim Your wonderful designs to others."

LEO THE GREAT
(?-461)

L EO was probably a native of Tuscany, but he considered himself a Roman. Rome to him was a holy city, and he protected it with the only weapon he had—a non-violent presence. He was the Pope and Bishop of Rome from 440 to 461.

The Roman Empire in his day was divided into East and West with two emperors, one in Constantinople (Istanbul) and one in Ravenna (in Italy). In the East, the empire was still relatively intact; the West was ravaged on its frontiers by invading German Tribes. Rome itself had been plundered in 410 by the Visigoths. Invaders settled in the Roman provinces and old social ways were breaking down.

Political Chaos Threatens the Church

Leo had a great concern for the Church. Political chaos threatened the Church. Western rulers at Ravenna could not protect their palaces. Many of the invading, settling Germans were Arians, members of a heretical movement denying the divinity of Christ. Pope Leo took the matter of widespread heresy in hand. He set about to extend the authority of the Roman Church and the Pope. He insisted that Christ exercised power on earth through Rome's bishop, successor to Peter to whom Jesus entrusted the "keys of the Kingdom." He consolidated Church authority in the West in himself, and by doing this he established a social and political structure—the Roman Catholic Church—bringing a sense of unity when the Roman Empire was gone.

Pope Leo's personality and his skill in settling disputes between politicians or prelates were great factors in his success in extending papal authority. His talent for diplomacy gave him a strong role in settling violent theological disputes within the Church. Centuries were needed to spell out doctrines and set up structures, though a core of orthodox teaching was determined usually by Church Councils across the first five centuries.

Leo's Meeting with Attila the Hun

Attila the Hun marched toward Rome, having already seized much of what was still called the Western Empire. Dressed in priest's robes rather than armor, and accompanied by a small band of Romans, the Pope went forth to meet the conqueror. Leo asked Attila to turn back, to spare the city. Surprisingly, the Hun agreed.

The Vandals arrived in 455 looking for spoils. Unable to persuade this horde to retire, Leo convinced its leader to pillage without burning the city. After two weeks of plundering, the Vandals departed for North Africa, taking with them numerous treasures of Rome's churches.

With strong conviction of the importance of the Bishop of Rome in the Church, and the Church as the ongoing sign of Christ's presence in the world, Leo displayed endless dedication in his role as Peter's successor, and in guiding his fellow bishops as "equals in the episcopacy and infirmities."

Leo is known as one of the best administrative Popes of the ancient Church, but his growth to sainthood had its basis in the spiritual depth with which he approached the pastoral care of his people. He is known for his spiritual profound sermons. Well versed in Scripture, Leo had the ability to reach the everyday needs and interests of his people.

Doctor of the Church

Speaking of Peter's words, "You are a holy priesthood, offering spiritual sacrifices which are acceptable to God through Jesus Christ," Saint Leo says in a sermon: "The Sign of the Cross makes kings out of those who are reborn in Christ and the anointing of the Holy Spirit consecrates them as priests. Hence, apart from the particular service of our ministry, all Christians who live according to the Spirit and according to the logic of their vocation must realize that they share a royal name and the office of the priesthood. For what is as royal as the fact that the spirit submissive to God is the guide of one's body? And what is as priestly as consecrating a

pure conscience to God and offering on the altar of one's
heart the spotless sacrifice of piety? . . . The Word made
flesh was now living among us and Christ offered Himself completely for the renewal of the human race."

Leo died in late 461. He is one of only three Popes
officially accorded the title "the Great" by the Catholic
Church, but not until the eighteenth century was he declared a "Doctor," a designation for the greatest theologians.

It is said that Leo's true significance rests in his
doctrinal insistence on the mysteries of Christ and the
Church and in the supernatural charisms of the spiritual
life given to man in Christ and in His body the Church.
Thus he held firmly that everything he did and said as
Pope for the administration of the Church was partici-
pated in by Christ, the head of the Mystical Body, and
by Saint Peter, in whose place he acted.

The feast day of Saint Leo the Great is celebrated
on November 10, on which the Church prays: "O God,
You established Your Church on the solid rock of Saint
Peter and You will never allow the powers of hell to
dominate her. Grant that she may persevere in Your
truth and enjoy continual peace through the intercession
of Pope Saint Leo."

DYMPHNA
(d. 620)

DYMPHNA was born in the seventh century, when Ireland was almost universally Catholic. Yet her father, Damon, a petty king of Oriel, was a pagan. Her mother was also of noble descent, exceptionally beautiful, and a devout Christian. Dymphna herself is said to have borne a striking resemblance to her mother.

Dymphna was fourteen when her mother died and her father is said to have been afflicted with a mental illness, brought on by his grief. When still very young, Dymphna, being filled with a deep love for Jesus Christ, chose Him for her Divine Spouse and consecrated her virginity to Him and to His Blessed Mother by a vow of chastity

Flight from Temptation

In a frantic effort to fill the void in his life caused by the death of his wife, Dymphna's father sent messengers throughout his own and other lands to find some woman of noble birth, resembling his beloved wife, who would be willing to marry him. Their search was fruitless. They directed the king's attention to the remarkable resemblance between Dymphna and her mother, and they dared to suggest that he propose marriage to her.

Under the stress of mental illness and passion, the king was willing to follow this scandalous proposal. He tried to persuade Dymphna by promises of riches and flattering words, but she was filled with disgust by the persistent advances of her father. Upon the advice of her confessor, Father Gerebran, she decided to flee from her homeland. He himself agreed to accompany her, together with two other friends.

The little group hurried to the coast. Faithful servants rowed them across the North Sea and they landed upon the Belgian coast near Antwerp, Holland. Fleeing inland, the fugitives made their way to Gheel. They found here a chapel dedicated to Saint Martin of Tours and decided to make their home near it. Dymphna soon made herself beloved by her tender care of the sick and poor.

Damon, very angry at the disappearance of his daughter, immediately set out in search of the fugitives. They were eventually traced to Belgium. In order to

break down Dymphna's resistance, the king gave orders
that Father Gerebran should be put to death. With one
blow of a sword his head was severed from his shoulders.

Martyrdom

Her father again tried to persuade his daughter to
return to Ireland with him. Infuriated by her resistance,
he drew his sword and struck off her head. She was then
only fifteen years of age. Dymphna received the crown
of martyrdom about the year 620.

The records of Dymphna's life and death say that
the bodies of the two martyrs were removed to a cave by
the inhabitants of Gheel. Some years later a more suit-
able burial place was sought. When the workingmen entered the cave and cleared away the rubble, they discovered two beautifully sculptured tombs of pure white
stone. They opened Dymphna's coffin and found lying
over her breast a red tile bearing the inscription: "Here
lies the body of the holy virgin and martyr, Dymphna."
Her remains were placed in a small church of the town
and later a shrine was erected over her remains. The
relics of her body were placed in a golden reliquary and
transferred to the magnificent church of St. Dymphna,
which was built upon the site of the original burial place.

Many miracles began to occur at Saint Dymphna's
shrine. Then began those strange pilgrimages of the de-
ranged to pray at her shrine. When they brought their
delusions and obsessions to be laid at the tomb of the
martyred virgin, they were tenderly cared for by the hos-
pitable villagers. Pilgrimages continued throughout the
Middle Ages. Gradually it became an established custom

for the pilgrims to remain in village homes while awaiting recovery.

The spot on which Saint Dymphna died at Gheel, Belgium, now houses one of the greatest medical centers in the world for the care and treatment of mentally sick people. Since the thirteenth century it has been their haven of refuge. But devotion began there in the seventh century. Sovereign Pontiffs and bishops and thousands of devoted Christians have always shown their veneration for Saint Dymphna as patroness of the nervous and emotionally disturbed.

Saint Dymphna's feast day is May 30, on which the Church prays: "Hear us, O God, our Savior, as we honor Saint Dymphna, patroness of those afflicted with mental and emotional illness. Help us to be inspired by her example and comforted by her merciful help."

BONIFACE
(680-754)

BAPTIZED Winfrid, Boniface was born in Wessex, a kingdom in the south of England, around A.D. 680, was educated in Benedictine monasteries, and became the headmaster of an abbey school near Winchester. Winfrid excelled as a scholar, writing one of the first Latin grammars prepared in England. He entered the Benedictine Order when he was thirty years old.

Once a priest he followed an inner urging into missionary work. He traveled to Rome in 718 with a group of pilgrims and there received his new name and a missionary commission from Pope Gregory II. He was to work east of the Rhine and to establish churches in keeping with Roman Catholic practice and administration.

Boniface Begins His Missionary Work

For three years Boniface worked in the Low Countries with a tribe of Saxons called Fresians. In 722 he was summoned to Rome for consecration as regional bishop for Germany. Pope Gregory gave him a letter of introduction to Charles Martel, the ruler of the Franks, a great hero who checked the advance of Islam in Europe, and the grandfather of Charlemagne, the first Holy Roman emperor. Martel liked Boniface and agreed to be his protector.

The missionary went into Germany, to Hesse. To undercut belief in the Teutonic gods, he assailed an oak tree to Thor, equivalent to the Greek god Zeus or the Roman Jupiter. "This god is no god," he declared, and proceeded to strike the old tree with an ax, until it came crashing to the ground.

The Church in Martel's Frankish kingdom was in a sorry condition. The ruler seized Church land and money at will; Church offices were auctioned to the highest bidders, and there was no set standard of Christian behavior. After Martel's death in 741, his successors were more cooperative. They sponsored a series of regional Councils that succeeded in restoring Church discipline.

In order to restore the Germanic Church to its fidelity to Rome, and to convert the pagans, Boniface had been guided by two principles. The first was to restore the obedience of the clergy to their bishops in union with the Pope of Rome. The second was the establishment of many houses of prayer which took the form of Benedictine monasteries. A great number of Anglo-Saxon monks and nuns followed him to the Continent. He introduced the Benedictine nuns to the active apostolate of education.

Christianity in eighth-century Europe was still testing itself, defining its course in relation to emerging political and social forces. Boniface believed the Church must first trust God, and then consistently follow its truth. In one of his letters he wrote: "In her voyage across the ocean of this world, the Church is like a great ship being pounded by the waves of life's different stresses. Our duty is not to abandon ship but to keep her on her course. Let us stand fast in what is right and prepare our souls for trial. Let us wait upon God's strengthening aid and say to him: 'O Lord, You have been our refuge in all generations.' "

Boniface's Death

For many years Boniface labored in Germany and France. But he could not forget that in Friesland there were still many pagans. He had done his work in Germany; there were many bishops there now to care for the Church. At the age of almost eighty, Boniface set out for his new mission field. In the first year he baptized many of the pagans. But there were others who would not listen to him and who were angry because of his success. Early in June, Boniface, with a number of other missionaries and an escort of Christians, went to meet a group of his new converts. As his party of 53 companions reached the meeting place, a crowd of his pagan enemies rushed upon him, overwhelmed his party, and killed them. Among the dead was Boniface, his head split by a sword. This happened on June 5 in 754.

Boniface bears out the Christian rule: to follow Christ is to follow the way of the Cross. For Boniface, it was not only physical suffering or death, but the painful, thankless, bewildering task of Church reform.

Saint Boniface is the patron saint of Germany. His feast is celebrated on June 5, on which the Church prays: "O Lord, let Saint Boniface intercede for us, that we may firmly adhere to the faith he taught, and for which he shed his blood, and fearlessly profess it in our works."

CYRIL AND METHODIUS
(d. 869, d. 885)

CYRIL was born in Thessalonica, northeast of Greece, and educated in Constantinople. He and his brother Methodius belonged to a senatorial family of Thessalonica, but their mother was probably a Slav.

Cyril was ordained a priest in Constantinople. He taught philosophy in the university and defended the Gospel of Christ.

The older brother, Methodius, after being governor of one of the Slavic colonies, became the abbot of a monastery in Greece.

A decisive change in their lives occurred when in 862, Ratislav, the Duke of Moravia, asked the Eastern Emperor, Michael III, to send him Christian missionaries to teach his people in their own language. Moravia is present-day Bohemia, Moravia, and Slovakia. He wanted political independence from German rule and ecclesiastical autonomy, that is, for Moravia to have its own clergy and liturgy. Cyril and Methodius undertook the missionary task.

The Two Brothers Become Missionaries

The two brothers were sent to the court of Ratislav at Velehrad. They both prepared Slavic liturgical texts in what would subsequently be known as the Cyrillic alphabet. It was formed from Greek capital letters. Together they translated the Gospels, the Psalter, Saint Paul, and the liturgical books into Slavic and composed the Old Slavonic liturgy.

That, and their free use of their native language in preaching, led to opposition from the German clergy. The bishop refused to ordain Slavic bishops and priests, and Cyril was forced to appeal to Rome. On the visit to Rome, they had joy of seeing their new liturgy approved by Pope Adrian II.

Cyril's Death

Cyril, long an invalid, died in Rome fifty days after taking the monastic habit.

An Old-Slavonic writing of Cyril's life describes his death in these words. "When the moment for rest had come, and the time to emigrate to the eternal dwelling, he raised his hands toward God and praying and weeping cried out: 'Lord, my God, You created the angelic orders and incorporeal spirits. You stretched out the heavens, made the earth firm, and called all things into being out of nothingness. You always hear those who do Your will and bear witness to You and observe Your precepts. Hear my prayer and keep in the faith Your flock over which You placed me Your unworthy and unsuitable servant.

" 'Deliver them from the impious and pagan malice of those who curse You, and let Your Church increase in number and gather all into one. Render Your people, the elect, harmonious in Your true faith and in the right confession and inspire in their hearts the word of Your doctrine. For it is Your gift that chose us to preach the Gospel of Your Christ, to inspire good works and accomplish what is pleasing to You.

" 'What You have given me I give back to You as Yours. Guide it with Your strong right hand, protect it in the shadow of Your wings so that all may praise and glorify Your Name of Father and Son and Holy Spirit. Amen.'

"Then after giving everyone a holy kiss, he said: 'Blessed be God who has not given us as food to the teeth of our invisible adversaries but has broken their snare and saved us from perdition.' Then at forty-two years of age he fell asleep in the Lord.''

Methodius Continues

Methodius continued mission work for sixteen more years. He was papal legate for the Slavic peoples, ordained bishop and then given an ancient see in present Yugoslavia. Though suffering much from detractors, he received assistance from Pope John VIII. He defended himself against charges of heresy and upheld his use of the Slavic liturgy. He was again vindicated.

Methodius died in Moravia, April 6, 885.

Saints Cyril and Methodius are honored as the apostles of the Slavs. Their feast day is celebrated on February 14, on which the Church prays: ''Merciful God, You have enlightened the Slavonic nations by the teaching of the brothers Cyril and Methodius. Help us to assimilate the teaching of Your doctrine and perfect us as a people united in the true faith and its expansion.''

BERNARD
(1091-1153)

IN the year 1091 Bernard was born in a castle in Burgundy, France. At an early age he was sent to the best schools where he remained till around age 19, during which time his mother died. He studied theology and Holy Scripture. After he finished his schooling and despite strong temptations of the flesh, he left his home to join the monastic community of Cîteaux. His five brothers, two uncles, and some 30 young friends followed him into the monastery.

Within four years a dying community was able to establish a new house in Champagne with Bernard as abbot. The zealous young man was quite demanding, though more on himself than others. A slight breakdown of health taught him to be more patient and understanding. The monastery was soon renamed Clairvaux, the valley of light.

Because of schisms which had arisen in the Church, Bernard traveled all about Europe restoring peace and unity. His ability as arbitrator and counselor became widely known. More and more he was lured away from the monastery to settle long-standing disputes. He was completely dedicated to the primacy of the Roman See. He intervened in a schism and settled it in favor of the Roman Pontiff against the antipope.

The Holy See prevailed on Bernard to preach the Second Crusade throughout Europe. His eloquence was so great that a large army was assembled. The ideals of the men and their leaders, however, were not those of Abbot Bernard, and the project ended in failure.

Devotion to Mary

Bernard's efforts produced far-reaching results. But he knew that they would have availed little without the many hours of prayer and meditation that brought him strength and heavenly direction. His life was characterized by a deep devotion to the Mother of God. His sermons and books about Mary are still the standard of Marian theology. He wrote: "In dangers, in doubts, in difficulties, think of Mary, call upon Mary. Let not her name depart from your lips, never suffer it to leave your heart. And that you may more surely obtain the assistance of her prayer, neglect not to walk in her footsteps. With her for your guide, you shall never go astray. While invoking her, you shall never lose heart. So long

as she is in your mind, you are safe from deception.
While she holds your hand, you cannot fall. Under her
protection you have nothing to fear. If she walks before
you, you shall not grow weary. If she shows you favor,
you shall reach the goal."

Bernard founded many monasteries. But he is
known more for his writings which have earned him the
title of the last of the Church Fathers and Doctor of the
Church.

On Love of God

Speaking of the love of God, Bernard wrote: "Love
is the only movement, feeling, or affection of the soul in
which the creature may, even if unequally, give answer
to the Creator and repay Him in kind. . . . For when
God loves, He wills only to be loved in return. . . .

"But the Bridegroom's love, or rather the Bridegroom who is love, looks only for faithful love in return.
The bride, then, must be allowed to love in return. How
can any bride, and most of all the bride of Love, do anything but love? How can Love not be loved? The bride,
then, rightly renounces all other feelings and gives herself wholly to love; she must respond to love by loving."

Bernard's greatest devotion was to Jesus Crucified
to whom he dedicated all his love. After a lifetime of
faithful service to Him, he died in the year 1153. His
feast day is August 20, on which the Church prays: "O
God, You blessed Your Church with Saint Bernard, a
man full of zeal for Your house, radiating brightness and
ardent love. Through his intercession, grant that we may
be animated by the same spirit and always walk as children of light."

DOMINIC
(1170-1221)

DOMINIC was born in modern Caleruega in what was the kingdom of Castile, Spain, in 1170. His father was a minor feudal lord. Young Dominic received a good education and in 1196 he became a canon in a community attached to the cathedral at Osma, where he later became a superior.

On a journey to northern Europe with his bishop, he came face to face with the Albigensian heresy. Its adherents taught that there were two opposing spirits in the universe, good and evil. All matter is evil, so they denied the Incarnation and the sacraments. Dominic was commissioned to be part of the preaching crusade against this heresy. Dominic, with three Cistercians, began traveling from place to place and preaching according to the Gospel ideal. He continued this work for 10 years. He was successful with the ordinary people but not with the leaders.

His fellow preachers gradually became a community, and in 1215 he founded a religious house at Toulouse which was to be the beginning of the Dominican Order. His ideal was to link a life with God, study, and prayer, with a ministry of salvation to people by the word of God, "to speak only of God or with God."

Pope Innocent III confirmed the Dominicans, who took the Rule of Saint Augustine as their pattern. Dominic inisisted on education for the preachers, and Dominican houses flourished around the great medieval universities.

From 1217 until his death in 1221, Dominic established his headquarters in Rome and made long journeys visiting the houses of the Order and preaching. There were sixty communities. He died with his mendicants, wandering and begging preachers, in Bologna. His dying request to the monks was: "Have charity among you, hold to humility, keep willing poverty."

Dominic's Visions

There is a legend that Dominic saw the sinful world threatened by God's anger but saved by the intercession of Our Lady, who pointed out to her Son two figures— Dominic himself and a stranger. In church the next day he saw a ragged beggar enter—the man in the vision. He went up to him, embraced him and said: "You are my companion and must walk with me. If we hold together, no earthly power can withstand us." The beggar was Francis of Assisi.

The Spanish founder of the great Dominican Order of Preachers was filled with the greatest admiration for the little barefoot Poor Man of God from Assisi. One year before Dominic's death the two were to meet once more at Our Lady of the Angels in Assisi and in Rome.

Dominic was very devoted to the Blessed Virgin Mary. The story is that once when Dominic became discouraged with the slow progress of his work of preaching against the Albigensian heresy in France, the Blessed Virgin appeared to him with a beautiful wreath of roses. She asked him to say the Rosary every day and to teach the people to say the Rosary. Soon the heresy began to disappear.

Dominic's Message

Dominic's message is clear. Acquired contemplation is the tranquil abiding in the presence of God and is an integral part of any full human Christian life. It must be the wellspring of all Christian activity. The effective combining of prayer and activity is the vocation of every good Catholic. Devotion to our Blessed Mother is an important means of imitating Christ and of obtaining the graces needed for sanctification. Dominic's way of honoring Mary was through the recitation of the Rosary.

Saint Dominic's feast day is August 8, on which the Church prays: "O God, let Saint Dominic help Your Church by his merits and teaching. May he who was an outstanding preacher of truth become a most generous intercessor for us."

FRANCIS OF ASSISI
(1181-1226)

FRANCIS was born in Assisi, Italy, in 1181. His father was Pietro di Bernardone, a prosperous seller of cloth. Young Francis learned a bit of Latin and French but was indifferent to school. Education meant less to him than spending money on good times with lively young friends. He was attracted by knighthood and military valor. At twenty he joined an Assisian campaign against neighboring Perugia, was captured, and spent almost two years as a prisoner of war.

Francis is Called

Probably ransomed by his family, Francis returned to his old life but soon fell ill. When he recovered he set

74

off on another military venture but in a dream a heavenly voice told him to go home "to serve the Master rather than the man." Assisi was no longer the same to him. He saw the emptiness of his frolicking life as leader of Assisi's youth. Prayer led him to a self-emptying like that of Christ. He wanted to be obedient to what he had heard in prayer: "Francis! Everything you have loved and desired in the flesh it is your duty to despise and hate, if you wish to know My will. And when you have begun this, all that now seems sweet and lovely to you will become intolerable and bitter, but all that you used to avoid will turn itself to great sweetness and exceeding joy."

From the Cross in the neglected field-chapel of San Damiano, Christ told him: "Francis, go out and build up My house, for it is nearly falling down." Francis would later interpret this as a command to shore up the walls of Christianity itself, but immediately it meant repairing San Damiano. He had already given away what he owned, so he generously helped himself to his father's fine cloth and sold it, taking the money to the priest at the old church.

His father accused his twenty-five-year-old son of theft. At a hearing before the local bishop, he was told to return the money. Francis obeyed and took off his own clothes, down to a hairshirt, returning them to Pietro and declaring: "I have called you father on earth, but now I say, 'Our Father, who art in heaven.' "

The Founding of an Order

For two years Francis lived a hermit's life near Saint Damian's, begging for his food and for the materials he used in repairing the old church. A few people began to realize that this man was actually trying to be Christian. He really believed what Jesus said: "Announce the Kingdom! Don't possess gold or silver or copper in your purses, no traveling bag, no shoes, no staff."

In 1209 Francis heard a sermon based on Jesus sending his disciples out to heal and preach, telling them to take no money or extra clothes. Francis had found his calling.

As he preached and practiced poverty in Assisi, Francis attracted followers, some of them, like himself, the sons of prosperous parents. His first Rule was a collection of texts from the Gospel. He had no idea of founding an Order, but once it began he protected it and accepted all the legal structures needed to support it. He has an absolute devotion and loyalty to the Church.

Francis was torn between a life devoted entirely to prayer and a life of active preaching of the Good News. He decided in favor of the latter but always returned to solitude when he could. The Order and its members were to be totally without possessions. In imitation of Christ they were to wander, preaching and helping people, neither taking money for their work nor paying for their keep.

In the early thirteenth century, both the Church and established religious orders were politically powerful, rich, and somewhat removed from the daily cares of the people, the vast majority of whom were peasants. The appearance of wandering, begging preachers concerned about everyday people fired imaginations.

The Franciscan Message

Early Franciscans brought a message of joy based on an awareness of the love of Christ. The heart of Francis' preaching was God's love demonstrated in the Cross. His stress on poverty and humility emerged from a theology of love. He did not say that money and other material goods are evil; he said that they divert attention from God. Humility, self-emptying to God, was for him the way to witness to the love of Christ in the world.

By 1210 the group around Francis had grown to a dozen. Francis went to Rome to ask permission to found an Order. Pope Innocent III was reluctant to approve new Orders. But convinced that Francis respected Church authority, the Pope gave his verbal blessing. A permanent Franciscan rule was written in 1220.

Francis called his Order the Humbler Brethren, or Friars Minor, and as the brothers moved north and south and beyond Italy in their brown robes, new recruits came from all directions. By 1219 they numbered 5,000

The Poor Clares

Clare Sciffo first heard Francis preach when she was sixteen years old. She sought his counsel and soon vowed to become a nun under his care. Her prominent family vigorously protested. On the night of Palm Sunday, 1211, she slipped away to the Franciscans at Our Lady of the Angels. She was not quite eighteen.

Francis first lodged Clare with a community of Benedictine nuns, then arranged a house for her and her sister next to Saint Damian's Church. Other women attracted to the Franciscan movement found their way to

Clare, and together with Francis she shaped the Order of Poor Clares. Clare sent groups of sisters to open new monasteries and new houses to care for the sick and the poor.

Francis' Last Years

Francis wanted to be a missionary in Syria and in Africa, but was prevented by shipwreck and illness in both cases. He did manage to try to convert the Sultan of Egypt during the Fifth Crusade. From Egypt he went to the Holy Land, where he received a message urging him to return to Italy. His brief absence had given those he left in charge enough time to begin transforming the Order into a traditional monastic community of established houses and educational centers. The Franciscan Order would not henceforth cling to absolute poverty. When the new Rule was approved in 1223 Francis withdrew from Franciscan affairs. He preached when he could, his health rapidly failing as a result of some diseases, including an eye ailment. Two years before his death, he received the stigmata, the real and painful wounds of Christ in his hands, feet, and side.

Francis died in his forty-fifth year, half-blind and seriously ill. On his deathbed, he said over and over again the last addition to his Canticle of the Sun: "Be praised, O Lord, for our Sister Death." He sang the 141st Psalm, and at the end he asked his superior to have his clothes removed when the last hour came. He then expired in imitation of his crucified Lord, October 4, 1226, as he prayed: "O Lord, I thank You for the pains which I suffer."

Francis of Assisi was poor only that he might be like Christ. He loved nature because it was another manifestation of the beauty of God. He did penance that he might be disciplined for the will of God in total dependence on the good God. The heart of his spirituality was living the Gospel life, summed up in the love of Jesus Christ, and perfectly expressed in the Holy Eucharist. His love for the Cross and the Eucharist is expressed: "We adore You, and we bless You, Lord Jesus Christ, here and in all the churches which are in the whole world, because by Your Holy Cross You have redeemed the world."

The feast of Saint Francis is celebrated on October 4 on which the Church prays: "O God, You enabled Saint Francis to imitate Christ by his poverty and humility. Walking in Saint Francis' footsteps, may we follow Your Son and be bound to You by a joyful love."

CLARE
(1193-1253)

CLARE was born at Assisi in 1193. She was the daughter of a count and countess. She heard Saint Francis preach in the streets of Assisi and told him of her desire to give herself to God. They became close friends.

On Palm Sunday, in the year 1212, the Bishop of Assisi presented a palm to this noble maiden of eighteen, who was beautifully dressed. That same night she left her beautiful home and went to the church of Our Lady of the Angels, where she met Francis and his Brothers. In that poor little chapel of the Portiuncula she received a rough woolen habit, exchanged her jeweled belt for a common rope with knots in it, and gave her life to Christ. She lived in an old Benedictine convent. Sixteen days later her sister Agnes joined her. Others came. They lived a simple life of great poverty and complete seclusion from the world, according to the rule Francis gave them as the Second Order. She started her Order of the Poor Clares. When she was 21, Francis obliged her under obedience to accept the office of abbess, in which she continued until her death.

Order of the Poor Clares

The nuns went barefoot, slept on the ground, ate no meat, and observed almost complete silence. But Clare persuaded her sisters to moderate this rigor. The greatest emphasis was on Gospel poverty. They possessed no property, even in common, subsisting on work and daily contributions.

Clare suffered serious illness for the last 27 years of her life in the convent of San Damiano in Assisi. Her influence was such that Popes, cardinals, and bishops often came to consult her—she herself never left the walls of the convent.

A well-known story concerns her prayer and trust. She had the Blessed Sacrament placed on the walls of the convent when it faced attack by invading Saracens. She prayed: "I beg You, dear Lord, protect these whom I am now unable to protect." To her sisters she said: "Don't be afraid. Trust in Jesus." The Saracens fled.

In a letter to Blessed Agnes of Prague, Clare wrote: "Happy indeed is she who is given the grace to share in the sacred banquet so that she may cling with all the fibers of her being to the One who holds the whole court of heaven spellbound with His beauty. Love for Him is exhilerating and the sight of Him renews our strength. His goodness fills our souls and His gentleness delights us. The recollection of Him provides us with pleasing light and His fragrance brings the dead to life. The vision of Him in glory will render blessed all the citizens of the heavenly Jerusalem. For He is the splendor of eternal glory, the refulgence of everlasting light, and a mirror without blemish.

"Look in this mirror every day, O queen and bride of Jesus Christ. Keep gazing at your image reflected in it so that you may be clothed and adorned with flowers of all virtues as becomes the daughter and chaste bride of the Most High. In this mirror blessed poverty, holy humility, and love beyond the power of words to describe are also reflected. And you will be able to contemplate them through the grace of God as in a perfect mirror. . . .

"As you meditate in this way, remember me, your poor mother, and be assured that I have inscribed your happy memory deeply on the tablets of my breast considering you dearer than all others."

Clare died in 1253 after a life of prayer, sacrifice, and devotion to the Holy Eucharist. Her feast day is August 11, on which the Church prays: "O God, in Your mercy You led Saint Clare to embrace poverty. Through her intercession, help us to follow Christ in the spirit of poverty and to contemplate You in the heavenly Kingdom."

ANTHONY OF PADUA
(1195-1231)

A NTHONY was born in Lisbon, Portugal, in 1195. His parents were very rich and wanted him to be a great nobleman. But the Gospel call to leave everything and follow Christ was the rule of his life. Over and over again God called him to something new in His plan. Each time Anthony responded with renewed zeal and self-sacrificing love to serve his Lord more completely.

As a very young man he decided to join the Augustinians, giving up a future of wealth and power to be a servant of God. Later, when the bodies of the first Franciscan martyrs were carried through the town where he

was stationed, he was again filled with an intense longing to be one of those closest to Jesus himself, those who
die for the Gospel. So Anthony entered the Franciscan
Order and set out to preach to the Moors. But an illness
prevented him from reaching his destination. He returned to Italy and was stationed in a small hermitage
where he spent most of his time praying, reading the
Scriptures, and doing menial tasks.

Preacher and Missionary

Anthony was a great preacher. He was sent out as
a missionary to many cities in Italy and France and converted many sinners and heretics. He was the first
member of his Order to teach theology to his brethren.
His sermons were notable for their learning and gentleness.

In his book of Sermons, Anthony says: "The saints
are like the stars. In His Providence Christ conceals them
in a hidden place that they may not shine before others
when they might wish to do so. Yet they are always
ready to exchange the quiet of contemplation for the
works of mercy as soon as they perceive in their heart
the invitation of Christ."

In another sermon Anthony says: "Whoever is filled
with the Holy Spirit speaks in many languages. 'Many
languages' are the various testimonies concerning Christ,
such as humility, poverty, patience, and obedience, with
which we speak when we exhibit these virtues to others
in our actions. Speech is alive when works also speak.
Let words cease, I beg you, and let works speak. . . .

"Let us therefore speak as the Holy Spirit may grant us to speak, begging Him humbly and devoutly to infuse His grace into us. May we thus bring the day of Pentecost to fulfillment by the perfect use of our five senses and the observance of the Ten Commandments. May we also be filled with a strong spirit of contrition and be on fire with the tongues of confession, so that blazing and illuminated we may be worthy to see the One and Triune God in the splendors of the Saints."

The Infant Jesus and Anthony

It is said that when Anthony was praying in his room, the Infant Jesus appeared to him, put His little arms around his neck, and kissed him. This wonderful favor was given to him because he kept his soul free from even the smallest sin and because he loved Jesus very much.

Anthony was only thirty-six years old when he died on June 13, 1231. Thirty-two years after his death his remains were brought to Padua. All the flesh except the tongue had been consumed by corruption. Many miracles took place after his death. Even today he is called the "wonder-worker."

Anthony's feast is celebrated on June 13, on which day the Church prays: "Almighty, ever-living God, You gave Your people the extraordinary preacher Saint Anthony and made him an intercessor in difficulties. By his aid grant that we may live a truly Christian life and experience Your help in all adversities."

BONAVENTURE
(1221-1274)

BONAVENTURE was born in the year 1221 at Bagnorea in Tuscany, central Italy. He was cured of a serious illness as a boy through the prayers of Francis of Assisi. He studied philosophy and theology at Paris. Inspired by Francis and the example of the friars, he entered the Franciscan Order. Having earned the title Master, he taught his fellow members of the Order of Friars Minor with great success.

Chosen as General of the Order in 1237, he was God's instrument in bringing the Order back to a deeper love of the way of Saint Francis, both through the life of Francis which he wrote at the request of his brothers and through other works in defense of the Order or in explanation of its ideals and way of life.

Bonaventure so united holiness and theological knowledge that he rose to the heights of mysticism while yet remaining a very active preacher and teacher, one beloved by all who met him.

Bonaventure became a close friend of Saint Thomas Aquinas and with him received the degree of Doctor of Theology. He also enjoyed the friendship of Saint Louis, King of France. Thomas asked Bonaventure one day where he had acquired his great learning. He replied by pointing to his crucifix.

The Seraphic Doctor

Bonaventure wrote many books. From the warmth of divine love which is found in his writings he is known as the "Seraphic Doctor," a seraph being a member of the highest order of angels.

In his book *The Journey of the Mind to God* he says: "Christ is the way and the door, the ladder and the vehicle; He is the 'mercy seat located above the ark of God' and 'the mystery hidden from all ages.' We must resolutely and fully direct our eyes toward Christ and look—with faith, hope, love, devotion, and admiration, exultation, thanksgiving, praise, and jubilation—on Him hanging from the Cross. We will thus celebrate the 'Passover' with Him, that is, we will set out to cross the Red Sea by means of the wood of the Cross. Leaving Egypt, we will enter the desert to taste therein the 'hidden manna' and remain with Christ in the tomb as if dead to external things. But we will really be experiencing—as much as is possible for us in our pilgrim state—what

Christ promised to the good thief: 'Today you will be with Me in paradise.' . . .

"Let us then pass over with the Crucified Christ 'from the world to the Father.' And when the Father shows Himself we will be able to say with Philip: 'It is enough for us' and hear with Paul the words: 'My grace is sufficient for you.' "

Last Days

Bonaventure was appointed by Pope Gregory X as Cardinal-Bishop of Albano, and he spoke first at the Second Council of Lyons. The morning of the 15th of July, 1274, in the midst of the Council, Pope Gregory X and the Fathers of the Council were shocked to learn that toward dawn Bonaventure had become ill and died.

An unknown chronicler has given his impression of the Franciscan cardinal: "A man of eminent learning and eloquence and of outstanding holiness, he was known for his kindness, approachableness, gentleness, and compassion. Full of virtue, he was beloved of God and human beings. At his funeral Mass that same day, many were in tears, for the Lord had granted him this grace, that whoever came to know him was drawn to a deep love for him."

Bonaventure's feast day is July 15, on which the Church prays: "Almighty God, today we celebrate the heavenly birthday of Saint Bonaventure, Your Bishop. Let us benefit by his wonderful teaching and always be inspired by his burning charity."

THOMAS AQUINAS
(1225-1274)

THOMAS was born in 1225. The family estate was near Aquino on the road from Rome to Naples. Nearby was the famous monastery of Monte Cassino. His feudal family intended him to become a cloistered monk. At five he was given to the Benedictine monastery by his parents who hoped that he would choose that way of life and later become abbot. Because of political disputes Monte Cassino was temporarily evacuated in 1239. Thomas, age 14, went home, and instead of returning to the monastery, enrolled at the new University of Naples to complete his studies. There he met Dominicans whose still young Order was committed to an educated clergy and was establishing houses at many universities. Thomas joined the Order when he was nineteen years old.

Thomas' family was unhappy because he had joined such a humble Order, so the young monk was kidnaped by his brother and held in confinement for more than a year. Unable to budge Thomas' determination, the family in 1245 allowed him to pursue is friar's life as a student in Paris. He studied with Saint Albert the Great, the teacher mainly responsible for introducing Aristotle into theology. After three or four years he accompanied Saint Albert to another teaching post in Cologne.

Thomas the Theologian

Returning to Paris in 1252 as student, then teacher, Thomas quickly became a major theological attraction of Europe. So great was his reputation that in 1259 he was called to Rome as lecturer and preacher to the papal court. He began his monumental work, *Summa Theologica,* during his nine years in Rome. It is a summation of Catholic theology. While the work was never finished, it was the most comprehensive statement of the Christian faith produced by the medieval world—the high point of Scholasticism, with its harmony of faith and reason.

Thomas returned to Paris in 1268 to engage over whether two truths, faith and reason, can be contradictory. He maintained that two truths cannot contradict one another. He insisted that within faith, reason can operate by its own law.

Debates between Thomas and his friend Saint Bonaventure took place in Naples, where Thomas went to 1272 to establish a Dominican house at the new university. Bonaventure disapproved of Thomas' heavy reliance on the philosophy of Aristotle.

Pope Gregory X sent for Thomas because his advice was needed in 1274 at the Council of Lyons, a meeting organized to heal the schism between Eastern and Western Christianity. Thomas set out, became ill on the road, and died on March 7, 1274, at a Cistercian abbey at Fossanova.

Faith and Reason

Thomas' greatest contribution to the Catholic Church is his writings. The unity, harmony, and continuity of faith and reason, of revealed and natural human knowledge, pervaded his writings. One might expect Thomas, as a man of the Gospel, to be an ardent defender of revealed truth. But he was broad enough, deep enough, to see the whole natural order as coming from God the Creator and to see reason as a divine gift to be highly cherished.

Thomas stopped work on the *Summa Theologica* after celebrating Mass on December 6, 1273. When asked why he stopped writing, he replied: "I cannot go on. . . . All that I have written seems to me like so much straw compared to what I have seen and what has been revealed to me." Thomas' writings fill sixty volumes. He built a new theological silo feeding Christian thought for centuries. Once asked if pride tugged at him, he replied in the negative, adding that common sense taught him that pride was unreasonable.

In addition to scholarly theology, Thomas wrote liturgical materials and hymns, many still used by

Churches of all denominations. He wrote the liturgical text for the Feast of Corpus Christi. His most popular hymn is the "Adoro Te," which begins with the words:

> Hidden God, devoutly I adore You,
> Truly present underneath these veils:
> All my heart subdues itself before You,
> Since it all before You faints and fails.

The last verse is:

> Contemplating, Lord, Your hidden presence,
> Grant me what I thirst for and more implore,
> In the revelation of Your essence.
> To behold Your glory evermore.

Canonized in 1323, Thomas was named a "Doctor" of the Catholic Church and is called the "Angelic Doctor." In 1879 Pope Leo XIII declared the *Summa* the basic instrument of Catholic teachings.

The feast of Saint Thomas Aquinas is celebrated on January 28. On that day the Church prays: "Father of wisdom, You inspired Saint Thomas Aquinas with an ardent desire for holiness and study of sacred doctrine. Help us, we pray, to understand what he taught and to imitate what he lived."

BRIDGET OF SWEDEN
(1303-1373)

BRIDGET was the daughter of the governor of the Swedish province of Upland. She was raised to be a feudal lady. She was married in 1316, when she was thirteen years old, to Ulf Gudmarsson, five years her senior, the son of another landed family and later a provincial governor. The couple lived happily together for twenty-eight years and had eight children.

In keeping with the practice of the day for noble women to serve as ladies-in-waiting to the Queen of Sweden, Bridget was called to the royal court in 1335. She was ill at ease as a glorified maid to Queen Blanche. She offered guidance to the new king, Manus II, and his

bride. Her visions, earlier concerned with spiritual matters, turned to politics. Stated as messages from God,
Bridget instructed the young rulers on how to conduct
affairs of state and to purify their faith in Christ.

A New Life

She left the royal court and went on a pilgrimage to
Spain with her husband. On the way back home, Ulf became sick. Husband and wife pledged to God that if he
should recover they would retire to the religious life.
They returned not to their feudal castle but to a monastery at Alvastra on Lake Vetter. There Ulf died and
Bridget stayed for four years as a penitent. She told of
frequent visions, especially of Christ crucified, to a
monastery superior, who recorded and translated them
into Latin.

Bridget then decided to found a religous community
at Vadstena. Her Order of the Most Holy Savior (Brigittines) included women and men, living in separate en-
closures. They shared the same church. The Brigittine
motherhouse became Sweden's literary center in the
fifteenth century.

Bridget wanted the Pope, then Clement VI, to return to Rome (the succession of Pontiffs was headquar-
tered temporarily in Avignon, a city in modern France).
In the Holy Year of 1350 she set off for Italy with a double purpose: to get a character for her Order and to en-
tice the papacy home. In 1370 the Brigittines finally got
a papal charter, but the Popes did not abandon Avignon
until four years after her death. Meanwhile, she kept
busy organizing charities for the poor and trying to
strengthen the monastic movement.

Hardship and Heartaches

Her life in Rome, where she was attended by her daughter, St. Catherine of Sweden, was filled with hardship and heartaches. She was often reduced to begging for food. Her favorite son, Karl disappointed her.

Bridget wrote many works in which she related her mystical experiences. A portion of her prayer to Christ our Savior reads: "My Lord Jesus Christ, may You be praised eternally for the time You hung on the Cross enduring the greatest sufferings and torments on behalf of us sinners. You felt the excruciating pain of Your wounds in Your very soul as well as in Your Most Sacred Heart, until it broke and You gave up Your spirit. Then bowing Your head You humbly entrusted Yourself into the hands of God Your Father and Your body experienced the coldness of death.

"Blessed may You be, my Lord Jesus Christ. You redeemed us with Your Precious Blood and Holy Death. And in Your merciful goodness You led us back from exile to eternal life."

A final pilgrimage to the Holy Land marred by shipwreck and the death of her son, Karl, eventually led to her death in Rome in 1373. Her body was taken in triumphal procession across Europe for burial at Vadstena. She was canonized less than twenty years later and named the patron saint of Sweden.

Her feast day is celebrated on July 23, on which the Church prays: "Lord God, You revealed heavenly secrets to Saint Bridget as she meditated on the Passion of Your Son. Grant that we Your servants may attain the joyful contemplation of Your glory."

CATHERINE OF SIENA
(1347-1380)

CATHERINE, the 23rd child of Jacopo and Lapa
Benincasa, was born in 1347 in Siena, Italy. She
grew up as an intelligent, cheerful, and intensely
religious person. Catherine disappointed her mother by
cutting off her hair, in protest against being overly encouraged to improve her appearance in the hope of at-
tracting a husband. Her father ordered her to be left in
peace, and she was given a room of her own for prayer
and meditation. At the age of twelve she took a vow of
virginity. Visions and voices summoned her to prayer
and physical austerity as means of spiritual discipline.
To prepare for membership in the Dominican Third

Order at 18, she confined herself for three years to a cavelike room under her father's leather and dye shop.

She emerged from isolation in 1366 in response to an urge to serve the sick and imprisoned in Christ's name. Catherine became a familiar sight in Siena, she in her white robe and black cape ministering to the poor and visiting the jails.

Catherine also taught, urging fortitude on any who would listen to her explanations of the courage needed to follow Christ in the world. Her accounts of spiritual visions and her acts of charity attracted a group of friend-followers.

Mystical Experiences

Catherine's mystical experiences inspired the *Book of Divine Doctrine,* the greatest writings on Christian mysticism of the fourteenth century. All of her writings soar with an awareness of the love and forgiveness of Christ. She conversed with God, who told her such things as why Christians must love neighbors:

"The soul that knows Me immediately expands to the love of her neighbor, because she sees that I love that neighbor ineffably, and so, herself, loves the object which she sees Me to have loved still more. She further knows that she can be of no use to Me and can in no way repay Me that pure love with which she feels herself to be loved by Me, and therefore she endeavors to repay it through the medium which I have given her, namely, her neighbor, who is the medium through which you can all serve Me."

In the early 1370's, Catherine turned increasingly to public and Church affairs beyond Siena. She particularly wanted to end the political conflict in Italy and for that to happen, she believed, the papacy had to return to Rome and direct the work of purifying the Church. Her initial efforts to persuade the reigning Pope, Gregory XI, to return from Avignon to Rome were by letter. She begged him to come home and clean up the Church. She denounced the material interests of cardinals and bishops and monasteries. Letters also poured forth to bishops, kings, and queens urging them to keep the true faith. Three secretaries were kept busy taking her dictation. She was jubilant when Pope Gregory returned to Rome.

She took to the road, talking peace to the belligerent Italian city states. She can be classified as a failed peacemaker, a naive mystic trying to translate ideas of union with God into the political scene, but her ideas lived on. Catherine made a strong argument for the Church to model peace by being peaceful.

Troubled Times for the Church

In 1378, the Great Schism broke out, splitting the allegiance of Christendom between two, then three, Popes. Catherine spent the last two years of her life in Rome, in prayer and pleading on behalf of the cause of Urban VI because she thought his election valid and, therefore, judged him the best hope of unifying the Church. She offered herself as a victim for the Church in its agony.

Catherine died at the age of thirty-three, surrounded by her "children," the simple people to whom she devoted herself.

Catherine ranks high among the mystics and spiritual writers of the Church. Her spiritual testament is found in *The Dialogue.* She wrote: "No persons should judge that they have greater perfection because they perform great penances and give themselves in excess to the staying of the body than those who do less, inasmuch as neither virtue nor merit consists therein. For otherwise that person would be an evil case, who from some legitimate reason was unable to do actual penance. Merit consists in the virtue of love alone, flavored with the light of true discretion, without which the soul is worth nothing."

The divine voice had told her: "In self-knowledge humble yourself; see that in yourself you do not even exist, for your very being, as you will learn, comes from Me, since I have loved both you and others before you existed." At twenty-three the heavenly voice upon which she relied for guidance told her: "You must go forth from your own city for the welfare of souls." She left the Tuscan city of her birth, to devote her last ten years to the tasks of building peace among the warring city states of Italy and unifying and purifying the Church in Western Europe. She accomplished neither, but she gained heroic stature in the efforts and was her century's brightest and best example of a life committed to Christ.

Saint Catherine's feast day is April 29, on which the Church prays: "O God, You caused Saint Catherine to shine with divine love in the contemplation of the Lord's Passion and in the service of Your Church. By her help, grant that Your people, associated in the mystery of Christ, may ever exult in the revelation of His glory."

ANGELA MERICI
(1470-1540)

ANGELA was born in 1470 in Desenzano in the territory of Lombardy. At fifteen years of age she became a tertiary of Saint Francis and lived a life of great austerity, wishing, like Saint Francis, to own nothing.

When she was twenty-two, Angela returned to her hometown to find that parents were not teaching their children the simplest truths of religion. She talked the matter over with her friends. They gathered together the little girls of the neighborhood to whom they gave regular instruction. Angela became the center of a group of people with similar ideals.

She eagerly took the opportunity for a trip to the Holy Land. When her group had gotten as far as Crete, she was struck with blindness. Her friends wanted her to return home, but she insisted on completing the pilgrimage visiting the sacred shrines. On the way back, while praying before a crucifix, her sight was restored at the same place where it had been lost.

A New Teaching Order

At 57, Angela organized a group of 12 girls to help her in catechetical work. In four years the group increased to 28. She formed them into the Company of Saint Ursula for the purposes of re-Christianizing family life through solid Christian education of future wives and mothers. The members continued to live at home, had no special habit, and took no formal vows, although the early Rule prescribed the practice of virginity, poverty, and obedience. The community thus existed as a "secular institute" until some years after Angela's death. She once said to her sisters: "If according to times and needs you should be obliged to make new rules and change certain things, do it with prudence and good advice." Angela has the double distinction of founding the first teaching order of women in the Church and what is now called a "secular institute" of religious women.

In her *Spiritual Testament,* Angela writes: "My most dear mothers and sisters in Christ, strive above all else and at any price to draw up wise resolutions with God's help. Thus, guided solely by love for God and zeal for the salvation of souls, you will carry out your task as educators.

"This task will bring forth fruits of salvation only if it is solidly grounded in love, for our Lord has said: 'A good tree cannot bring forth bad fruits.' He says, a good tree—that is, a good heart, animated by love—can bring forth only good and holy fruits. That is why Saint Augustine used to say: 'Love, and then do what you will.' Have love and charity, and then do what you will. He was saying, as it were, Love cannot sin. . . .

"Therefore my most dear mothers, if you love your daughters with an ardent and sincere charity, it will be impossible for you not to have every single one of them engraved in your heart.

"I also ask You to try to draw them by love, compassion, and charity rather than by pride and harshness. Be sincerely kind to all in accord with this word of our Lord: 'Learn from Me, because I am meek and humble of heart.' Thus You will be imitating God, about whom it is written: 'He has arranged all things sweetly.' And again Jesus said: 'My yoke is easy and My burden light.'

"Furthermore, use pleasantness toward all in its manifold forms. Take especial care to insure that it is not out of fear that they obey what You command. God has bestowed freedom on everyone, and so He forces no one. He is content to demonstrate, call, persuade. At times, it is true, you must show a more stern authority, in a good way and in accord with the state and the needs of individuals. However, even then it is only charity and zeal for souls that should motivate us."

Angela died in 1540. Her feast day is January 27, on which the Church prays: "O Lord, let Saint Angela never cease commending us to Your kindness. By always imitating her charity and prudence may we succeed in keeping Your teachings and preserving good morals."

THOMAS MORE
(1477-1535)

THOMAS More was born in 1477 and was educated at Oxford. He married and had one son and three daughters.

Thomas was one of the best-known men in Europe. He had been a lawyer first as his father had been before him, and then a sheriff of London, a member of Parliament and of the king's council. The king of England,

Henry VIII, made him Lord Chancellor of England. His
reputation did not depend upon his political positions.
His writings alone were enough to make him famous,
and he was a friend and teacher to every learned man of
Europe.

But his close friends knew other things about him:
how he loved to tease and joke, how he loved fun and
music and laughter, how kind he was to his family, and
how he had taken poorer relatives to live with him even
when he had none too much money for his own family.
His friends knew also that at one time he had thought of
becoming a priest, that, while studying law, he had lived
for four years in a monastery so that he could see just
how the monks lived, and that he had been advised by
his confessor to give up the idea of the priesthood,
marry, and live a good life in the world.

Thomas tried to make use of his keen mind for all
good causes. His piety and his love for the priesthood he
had never given up. Very often his splendid court dress
hid a hair-shirt, and very often, too, he was hungry because of his strict fasts. Everyone could see that he was
very regular at the sacraments and faithful to daily
Mass.

Thomas Refuses To Take an Oath

One day a courtier whispered to Thomas as he was
participating in Holy Mass: "My Lord, His Majesty the
king wishes you to come to him at once."

The chancellor replied: "I cannot come now. Say to
the king for me that I am paying court to a greater King
than he. My duty to the Greater done, I shall await upon

His Majesty at once." The man left and the chancellor prayed devoutly until the end of Mass.

The king Henry VIII had become tired of his wife Catherine and had for some time been trying to get the Pope to grant a divorce so that he might marry a maid, Anne Boleyn. The Pope naturally would not consent.

The king had a law passed by a weak Parliament making him head of the Church of England and demanding that the bishops and priests take an oath recognizing him as their superior. Thomas More could not take the oath and be true to his conscience, so he resigned his office as chancellor.

He was summoned to appear before the court at Lambeth to take the oath. Thomas went to Mass and received Communion and then set out for Lambeth. When the court found that he could not be forced to take the oath, it had him imprisoned. Later he was taken to the Tower of London and ultimately tried for treason.

In a letter written in prison to his daughter Margaret, Thomas wrote: "I know the unworthiness of my past life, which deserves that God abandon me. Yet I can only trust in His merciful goodness, for it is His grace that has strengthened me up to the present. It has helped me to give up my goods, my lands, and even my life rather than to swear against my conscience. . . .

"Margaret, I also know very well that barring some fault on my part God will never abandon me. I shall therefore entrust myself wholly to Him in good hope. And if He should allow me to perish because of my fault, I shall at least serve to gain Him praise for His justice. But I trust that His tender pity will keep my poor soul safe and make me serve to demonstrate His mercy rather than His justice. . . . Do not be troubled by anything that can overtake me in this world. Nothing can happen without God allowing it. And all that He allows, no matter how bad it may seem, is truly for the best.''

Martyrdom

Thomas was led out of the prison and came before the scaffold, weak from his long imprisonment. He prayed for a while, then bound a cloth about his own eyes, and laid his head upon the block. The ax came down with a thud, and Thomas, the greatest man of his time, was dead. This happened on June 6, 1535, on Tower Hill, London.

His belief that no lay ruler has jurisdiction over the Church of Christ cost Thomas More his life. He steadfastly refused to approve Henry VIII's divorce and remarriage and establishment of the Church of England. Nor would he acknowledge Henry as supreme head of the Church in England, breaking with Rome and denying the Pope as head. Upon conviction, Thomas declared he had all the Councils of Christendom and not just the council of one realm to support him in the decision of his conscience.

Four hundred years later, in 1935, Thomas More was canonized a saint of God. A supreme diplomat and counselor, he did not compromise his own moral values in order to please the king, and for this the Church points to him as an example of loyalty to God and his Church, and as a devoted father to his family.

On his feast day, June 22, the Church prays: "O God, You will that the witness of martyrdom should be

the finest expression of the faith. Through the intercession of Saint Thomas, grant that we may confirm by the
testimony of our lives that faith which we profess with
our tongue."

IGNATIUS LOYOLA
(1491-1556)

IGNATIUS was born in 1491 at Loyola in Cantabria,
Spain. He spent his early years at court and as a
soldier.

Ignatius was on his way to military fame and for-
tune at the age of thirty when a cannonball shattered his
leg. Because there were no romantic books about
knights on hand during his convalescence, he whiled

away the time reading a life of Christ and lives of the saints. To his own surprise he found himself getting interested. He decided to try to do what the saints had done.

The doctor finally told him that he needed no further care. Ignatius left the castle in which he had been convalescing, looked for a priest, and went to confession. A few days later he gave away his fine clothes and dressed himself in the oldest things he could find. For almost a year he lived in a cave on the banks of the river at Manresa. He had punished himself for his sins—fasting for days, whipping himself, and taking care of the poor and sick. He then decided to go to Jerusalem to help the poor Christians there who were persecuted by the Turks, but the Turks would not allow him to stay and so he returned to Spain.

In Barcelona he entered school—a man 35 years old, in the lowest class and among the youngest students. After some years here he was ready for the University, and he went to Paris. All this time he was doing what he could in his spare time in hospitals and among the poor. He got other students interested in this work, but after some time they fell away.

The Society of Jesus

In the year 1534, though, he had five faithful followers and with these he formed a little Society. They offered themselves to the Pope for any work he wanted them to do. Ignatius saw the world as a big battlefield. Just now there was a battle raging: Luther and the other Reformers had drawn their swords against the old

Church, and whole countries were falling away from the faith. As soon as Ignatius saw his work ahead of him, he formed with the first five followers the Society of Jesus. It was the beginning of the Jesuit Order. Arguing, pleading, preaching, praying, teaching, he saw his men do great work for the Church all over the world. It was his Order that finally turned the tide against the Protestant Reformers and started Europe back toward the Church. His men were in the mission field everywhere. Even in the forests of America his men were teaching the faith to savage Indians. Our own American saints, Isaac Jogues, John Brebeuf and the others martyred with them, were Jesuits. They were among the first to carry the faith to North America. Our first bishop, John Carroll, was a Jesuit.

The Patron of Retreats

Ignatius was a true mystic. He centered his spiritual life on the essential foundations of Christianity—the Trinity, Christ, the Eucharist. His motto was, "All for the greater glory of God." He is the patron of retreats. Ignatius recommended this prayer to his penitents: "Lord Jesus Christ, take all my freedom, my memory, my understanding, and my will. All that I have and cherish You have given me. I surrender it all to be guided by Your will. Your grace and Your love are wealth enough for me. Give me these, Lord Jesus, and I ask for nothing more."

He exercised a most fruitful apostolate both through his written works and through his training of followers who won great praise for their renewal of the Church.

He wrote: "Great care must be taken to show forth orthodox truth in such a way that if any heretics happen to be present they may have an example of charity and Christian moderation. No hard words should be used nor any sort of contempt for their errors be shown."

For fifteen years Ignatius directed the battles of his Society. His men wanted him for their general. Almost blind, worn out by his hard life and prayer, he died at the age of sixty-five on July 31, 1556.

On his feast day, July 31, the Church prays: "O God, You raised up Saint Ignatius in Your Church to inspire men to work for Your greater glory. Grant that we may labor on earth with his help and after his example may merit to be crowned with him in heaven."

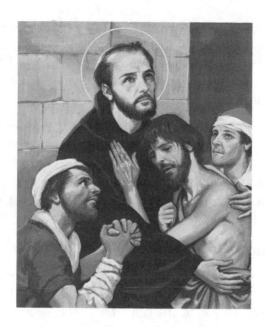

JOHN OF GOD
(1495-1550)

JOHN was born in Monte-mayor-el-Novo, in Portugal, in 1495. His parents were poor and very religious. When he was eight years of age he was kidnaped. He found himself an outcast in Castile, on the Spanish peninsula. He settled down as a shepherd-boy in the neighboring countryside and remained there until he was twenty-two years of age.

This was an era of wars and conquests. John joined a company of soldiers and fought for the emperor Charles V, first against the French and later in Hungary against the Turks. For eighteen years he was employed as a soldier in various parts of Europe. He lost whatever faith and devotion he once possessed. He laid aside his morals; he was ashamed to be thought better than his fellow soldiers. But no matter how wild his life might have been, John had always a soft spot in his heart for the poor and suffering.

John was forty years of age when his regiment was at last disbanded. Immediately he set about making something of himself. He went on a pilgrimage and put himself right before God by a good confession. He was determined that in some way the rest of his life should be spent in atonement.

A New Life

He returned to Spain and found work as a poor shepherd once more. Compassion for the distressed led him to leave his job in the hope that by crossing to Africa he might comfort and help the Christian slaves detained there. At Gibraltar he met a Portuguese gentleman whose estates had been confiscated. John was so full of pity for this exile and his wife and children that he sold all he had and helped support this family. He even hired himself out as a day-laborer at the public works in order to earn a little money for their benefit.

John went to Granada where he opened his own store and there sold pictures and pious objects. Later he went on a pilgrimage to Our Lady of Guadalupe, and there he discovered his true vocation. He came back to Granada, rented a house, and began to gather in it all the sick, poor, and homeless people of the town. He would wash his patients and dress their sores; he would sit by their side and encourage them, and then he would urge them to go to confession and to pray.

John considered himself bound to try to help every distressed person he heard about. He organized strict inquiries into the needs of the poor and sick throughout the whole province, relieved some in their homes, provided work for others, and made the greatest sacrifices to comfort and assist all the afflicted members of Christ. Crucifix in hand, he would often seek out hardened sinners and would exhort them to repentance.

A Beggar for the Poor

To maintain his hospital, John went out to beg, rattling a tin can in his hand, shouting as loud as charity would allow him. Very soon there grew up about his house a group of more wealthy men and women who took pride in calling themselves his benefactors. The Archbishop of Granada gave him the name of "John of God" and prescribed a kind of habit for him.

Although his life seemed to be one of continual action, John accompanied it with frequent prayer and self-sacrifice. His charity was fed and inflamed by frequent meditation on the sufferings of Christ, to whom he often used to say: "Lord, Your thorns are my roses and Your sufferings my paradise."

In one of his letters John wrote: "Whenever I see so many people who are poor and those who are my neighbors suffering beyond their forces and afflicted with so much pain both in soul and in body that I cannot assuage, I am overcome with sadness. But I place my trust in Christ, for He knows my heart. That is why I say: 'Accursed is the person who places his trust in human beings rather than in Christ alone.' For—whether you want it or not—you will be separated from humans. But

Christ is faithful and is always with us, for He provides all things. Let us give thanks to Him at every moment."

Worn out by fifteen years' hard service in behalf of the sick, John died a victim of charity. The cause of his illness was overexhaustion. His acts of mercy in the service of the sick and poor had proved too much of a strain on his heart. On March 8, 1550, the nurses found the saint dead, still kneeling, his face resting on the crucifix. He was canonized in 1690. In 1886 Pope Leo XIII declared him the heavenly patron of all hospitals and the sick. His feast is celebrated on March 8, on which the Church prays: "O God, You filled Saint John with the spirit of compassion. Grant that by practicing works of charity we may deserve to be numbered among the elect in Your kingdom."

FRANCIS XAVIER
(1506-1552)

FRANCIS was born in 1506 in Spain of noble parents. He was sent to the College of Saint Barbara in Paris and became a teacher of philosophy. He had a highly promising career in academics.

Francis was 24 when he met Ignatius of Loyola, who often repeated to him the word of Our Lord: "What profit is it to a man if he gain the whole world, and lose his soul?" After tireless persuasion Ignatius finally won the young man to Christ. Francis made the spiritual exercises under the direction of Ignatius and in 1534 joined the Society of Jesus. Together at Montmartre they vowed poverty, chastity, and apostolic service, according to the directions of the Pope.

From Venice, where he was ordained a priest in
1537, he went on to Lisbon and from there sailed to the
East Indies. He landed at Goa, on the west coast of
India. For the next ten years he labored to bring the
faith to the Hindus, the Malayans and the Japanese.

A Life of Poverty

Wherever he went, he lived with the poorest people,
sharing their food and rough accommodations. He spent
countless hours ministering to the sick and the poor,
particularly to lepers. He converted thousands of
pagans. In one of his letters to Ignatius he wrote: "Since
I arrived here, I have not had a moment's respite. I continually toured the villages, baptizing all the children not
yet baptized. . . . In these places many do not become
Christians for the sole reason that they lack those to
make them Christians. Many times I think about making
a tour of European universities, especially those in Paris,
running and crying out all around like a madman, and
arousing those who have more learning than charity
with these words: 'How many souls because of you are
excluded from heaven and cast into hell!' "

Francis went through the islands of Malaysia, then
up to Japan. He learned enough Japanese to preach to
simple folk, to instruct, and to baptize, and to establish
missions. From Japan he had dreams of going to China,
but this plan was never realized.

Devotion to Mary

Francis venerated Mary, the Mother of God, all his
life with deep tenderness. When he implored God for

any grace, it was done through her intercession. He always exhorted the faithful to have recourse to her and concluded all his sermons with the "Hail, Holy Queen." He considered it an honor to show exteriorly that he was Our Lady's servant and to wear around his neck the Rosary, which he said daily, and which he used for the performance of some of his miracles whereby many unbelievers were converted.

Francis had a special devotion to the Immaculate Conception of the Blessed Virgin and made a vow to defend and spread this truth of faith with all his energy. When on his missionary travels he met great sinners, he fervently prayed to the Mother of mercy to obtain for them the grace of conversion. When the hour of death approached, he appealed to Mary with fervor, often repeating the words, "Show yourself a Mother."

Francis died on the island of Sancian, a hundred miles southwest of Hong Kong, on December 2, 1552. In his final sickness he had to be removed from the ship because the Portuguese sailors feared that kindness to him would offend their master. They left him on the sands of the shore, exposed to a bitter wind, but a Portuguese merchant brought him into a hut. He prayed continually, but he grew weaker. His friend, Anthony, wrote later: "I could see that he was dying, and I put a lighted candle in his hand. Then, with the name of Jesus on his lips, he gave his spirit to his Creator and Lord with great peace and repose."

Francis Xavier is the patron of the foreign missions. His feast day is celebrated on December 3, on which the Church prays: "O Lord, You won many peoples for Your Church through the preaching of Saint Francis. In-

spire the faithful today with the same zeal for spreading
the faith, so that everywhere the Church might rejoice in
her many children."

CHARLES BORROMEO
(1538-1584)

CHARLES Borromeo was born at Arona in Lombardy
on October 2, 1538. Although he belonged to a
noble Milanese family and was related to the powerful Medici clan, he desired to devote himself to the
Church. When his uncle, Cardinal de Medici, was
elected Pope in 1559 as Pius IV, he made Charles cardi-
nal-deacon and administrator of the archdiocese of
Milan while he was still a layman and a young student.
Because of his intellectual qualities Charles was entrusted with several important offices connected with the

Vatican and later appointed Secretary of State with full charge and soon afterward he was ordained Bishop of Milan.

As a true pastor of his flock he tirelessly promoted Christian life by the reform of his diocese. Specific regulations were drawn up for bishops and other clergy because he was convinced that if the people were to be converted to a better life, the clergy had to be the first to give a good example and renew their apostolic spirit.

A Man of Action

Charles became a great reformer and, more than anyone else, helped the Church during the storm caused by Martin Luther at the time of the Reformation. His great work was the direction of the Council of Trent and the carrying out of its decrees. He founded schools for the poor, seminaries for clerics, and through his community of Oblates trained his priests to holiness of life. He instructed Saint Aloysius Gonzaga, heard his confession, and gave him his First Holy Communion.

Charles founded hospitals where he himself served the sick. He slept on straw or boards and lived on black bread, chestnuts, and dried figs. He was often seen taking part in public processions with a rope around his neck as a sign of penance.

Charles had a great love for the poor. He gave away all his belongings and wore an old patched cloak. During the great plague, he was ever with the sick and dying. He made his own the words of Christ: "I was hungry and you gave Me food, I was thirsty and you gave Me to drink. I was a stranger and you welcomed

Me, naked and you clothed Me. I was ill and you comforted Me, in prison and you came to visit Me" (Mt 25:35-37). He saw Christ in his neighbor and knew that his charity for the least of his flock was charity done for Christ.

A Man of Words

In a sermon given during the last synod he attended at Milan, Charles said: "My brothers, you must understand that nothing is more necessary for churchmen than mental prayer—it must precede, accompany, and follow all our acts. 'I will sing,' says the Prophet, 'and I will be attentive.' My brother, when you administer the sacraments, be attentive to what you are doing. When you celebrate Mass, reflect on what you are offering. When you chant the Office in choir, think about the Lord to whom you are speaking and the words you are saying. When you direct souls, remember the Lord's Blood that has made them clean. Thus, let everything you do be done with love.

"In this way we will overcome the countless difficulties that we necessarily encounter every day because of our office. And in this way we will obtain the strength to bring forth Christ in ourselves and in others."

What he says about the importance of meditation in the life of a priest would certainly apply to the life of the laity in their own circumstances. In meditation and prayer all Catholics will find the strength to bring Christ to birth in themselves and in those whose lives they touch.

Work and the heavy burdens of Charles' high office began to affect his health. He died in 1584 at the age of 46. His feast day is November 4, on which the Church prays: "O God, maintain in Your people that spirit with which You inspired Your Bishop, Saint Charles, so that Your Church may be constantly renewed, conforming itself to Christ and manifesting Christ to the world."

JOHN OF THE CROSS
(1542-1591)

JUAN de Yepes Alvarez was born at Fontiveros in Spain in 1542. His parents were very poor. He became the servant of the poor in the hospital of Medina. At twenty-one he became a lay brother at a Carmelite monastery where he practiced severe penance. His superiors, knowing his talents, sent him to

Salamanca for higher studies, and he was ordained a priest at twenty-five.

He met Saint Teresa of Avila, who interested him in the work of reforming his own Order. As a partner with Teresa, and in his own right, John engaged in the work of reform. Imprisoned by unreformed Carmelites he became the first prior or superior of the Discalced or barefoot Carmelites as John of the Cross. He came to know the Cross, to know the dying of Jesus, as he sat month after month in his dark, narrow cell with only his God. He experienced opposition, misunderstanding, persecution, and imprisonment. Yet in this slow death of imprisonment John came into the light. After nine months of suffering, he escaped. On two other occasions he was publicly disgraced.

John wrote: "Live in the world as if only God and your soul were in it; then your heart will never be made captive by any earthly thing." Since he was always united to God in sincerest love, he bore his sufferings patiently.

A Mystic-Poet

John was a mystic-poet, expressing the ecstasy of mystical union with God in his books *Spiritual Canticle,* and *Ascent of Mount Carmel.* He wrote about the path to union with God: rigorous discipline, abandonment, and purification. He taught that the Cross leads to resurrection, agony to ecstasy, darkness to light, abandonment to possession, denial of self to union with God.

In his *Spiritual Canticle* John of the Cross writes: "It is necessary for us to dig deeply into Christ. He is like an inexhaustible mine which has so many hidden pockets of treasure that we never reach the bottom, no matter how deeply we dig. In every corner there are found, here and there, new veins of new wealth.

"For this reason the Apostle Paul said that in Jesus 'every treasure of wisdom and knowledge is hidden.' The soul cannot reach these treasures; nor can it become capable of reaching them unless it has first passed and gone through a multitude of difficulties, suffering internally and externally, and unless it has first received many intellectual and sensible gifts from God, and unless there has first been a long spiritual training. . . . All these things indeed are subordinate and simple dispositions for the sublime penetration of the knowledge of the mysteries of Christ—which is the highest wisdom."

Disciples of the Cross

The story of John's life is summed up in the words: "If anyone wishes to follow Me, let him deny himself and take up his cross daily." The Paschal Mystery— through death to life—strongly marks John as a reformer, mystic-poet and theologian-priest. He has a crucial word for us today. We tend to be rich, soft, and comfortable. We shrink even from the words self-denial, purification, and discipline. His message is: Do not run from the Cross if you really want to live!

John was one of the great contemplatives. He was declared a Doctor of the Church. He died in 1591.

His feast day is December 14, on which the Church prays: "O God, Your Priest Saint John became a model of perfect self-denial and showed us how to love the Cross. May we always imitate Him and be rewarded with the eternal contemplation of Your glory."

VINCENT DE PAUL
(1581-1660)

VINCENT was a farm boy born at Pouy, France, in 1581. He alone of eight children showed an interest in education. His father sold a yoke of oxen to send Vincent to school at Dax. Then came theological studies at the University of Toulouse. He was ordained in 1600.

The popular story says that Vincent was captured by Barbary pirates, sold as a slave, and suffered abuse until he converted his master. His work was among convicted criminals sent to the galley as oarsmen. He treated them with special compassion and kindness. He demanded and got better dungeons for them onshore, looked after their medical needs, and ministered to their souls. It is said that he ransomed as many as twelve hundred Christians enslaved in Africa.

Later Vincent appeared in Paris, possibly as chaplain to Queen Margaret of Valois. His inclinations seemed to be toward worldly comforts until he came under the influence of Cardinal Pierre de Berulle, a mystic. He sent Vincent as tutor to the children of Count Philip de Gondi, master of the French fleet and a large estate holder.

The Vincentians

The deathbed confession of a dying servant opened Vincent's eyes to the crying spiritual needs of the peasantry of France. It was Countess de Gondi, whose servant he helped, who persuaded her husband to endow and support a group of able and zealous missionaries who would work among the poor, the vassals and tenants, and the country people in general.

Vincent was too humble to accept leadership at first, but after working for some time in Paris among imprisoned galley-slaves, he returned to be the leader of the Congregation of the Mission, or the Vincentians. These priests, with vows of poverty, chastity, obedience, and stability, were to devote themselves entirely to the people in smaller towns and villages. Later they became very active in foreign missionary work.

The Sisters of Charity

Subsequently Vincent established confraternities of charity for the spiritual and physical relief of the poor and sick of each parish. From these, with the help of

Saint Louise de Marillac, came the Sisters of Charity, "whose convent is the sickroom, whose chapel is the parish church, whose cloister is the streets of the city." Louise, canonized by the Church in 1934, was a widow who did much of the day-to-day work of organizing and running the Order.

Vincent's original idea was to form a group, not an Order of sincere aristocratic women to serve the poor. He was an able recruiter. Titled ladies, who had to prepare themselves spiritually, put on grey frocks for visits of mercy to poorhouse and prison. Vincent set the movement's spiritual tone—he prayed hourly—and took part himself in the lowly labor.

Many nurses and new institutions were needed to help the poor. Louise de Marillac moved the Sisters of Charity from a lay movement into a religious Order, but in 1642, nine years after Louise opened a training program in her home, Vincent permitted the Sisters of Charity to take vows of poverty, obedience, and chastity in order to educate and assign widows and peasant girls to the work of helping the poor. In 1655 the Order was formally established.

Vincent was zealous in conducting retreats for clergy at a time when there was great laxity, abuse, and ignorance among them. He was a pioneer in clerical training and was instrumental in establishing seminaries.

Love for the Poor

Vincent was by temperament a very hot-tempered person. He said that except for the grace of God he would have been "hard and repulsive, rough and cross."

But he became a tender and affectionate man, very sensitive to the needs of others: He wrote: "We must take care of the poor and offer them comfort, help, and support. Accordingly, Christ willed to be born poor, selected poor men as His Apostles, became the servant of the poor, and shared the condition of the poor. Christ did this so completely that He stated He would consider any good or evil done to the poor as done to Himself."

Vincent showed his compassion and love for individual souls he came in contact with in his ministry of charity. In a letter he wrote: "Strive to live content in the midst of those things that cause your discontent. Free your mind from all that troubles you; God will take care of things. You will be unable to make haste in this [choice] without, so to speak, grieving the heart of God, because He sees that you do not honor Him sufficiently with holy trust. Trust in Him, I beg you, and you will have the fulfillment of what your heart desires."

Vincent de Paul died in the fall of 1660 as he sat quietly in a chair. His life teaches that the greatest concern of the Church must be for those who need the most help—those made helpless by sickness, poverty, ignorance, or cruelty. He is a particularly appropriate patron for all Christians today, when hunger is becoming starvation, and the high living of the rich stands in more and more glaring contrast to the physical and moral degradation in which many of God's children are forced to live.

The feast of Saint Vincent de Paul is September 27. The Church prays: "O God, You gave Saint Vincent de Paul apostolic virtues for the salvation of the poor and the formation of the clergy. Grant that, endowed with the same spirit, we may love what he loved and act according to his teaching."

TERESA OF JESUS
(1515-1582)

TERESA was born in 1515. Her father was a gentleman of Avila, the beautiful fortress town in central Spain; her mother died when Teresa was twelve years old. Her late teen years were divided between lying sick at home and living in a convent, first as a student, then as a novice.

Teresa's major work did not begin until she was past forty. After a religious experience in which an angelic apparition pierced her heart filling her with pain and delight, she was ready to do whatever Christ commanded. She wrote: "I am Yours. I was born for You. What do You, Master, want to make of me? It is You alone who live in me. What do You desire that I should do for You?"

Her service to Christ and the Church would be to return the Carmelite Order in Spain to its original simplicity and austerity.

Reform of the Carmelites

The Carmelites formed one of the great new religious movements in the Middle Ages. An order of hermits began in the late twelfth century on Mount Carmel in Palestine. The formal order of Carmelite nuns was begun in 1452. The Carmelites lost much of their original vigor and fervor and also acquired property. Teresa came to consider her own convent too lax and too dependent on revenues. She believed that nuns should live from alms and go shoeless.

In 1562, Teresa opened her own convent, called Saint Joseph's for shoeless (or discalced) Carmelite nuns. Her nuns wore coarse brown habits and veils, slept on straw, ate no meat, and rarely if ever left the cloister. For five years Teresa was the mother superior of Saint Joseph's, schooling the nuns in the way of prayer and self-sacrifice.

In 1567 the Carmelite officials in Rome approved her reform. She moved across Spain, founding discalced communities, usually of only thirteen women each. On her travels she met Juan de Yepes, better known as John of the Cross, a young Carmelite priest, who became Teresa's chief collaborator in reform and in the spread of Spanish mysticism. John wrote numerous spiritual books which traced the mystic's path to God.

A Woman for God

Both Teresa and John were accused of pride by opponents of their Carmelite reform. She was misrepresented to the Order's general and was directed to cease founding new convents. King Philip II of Spain intervened for Teresa and John, and a division was effected between the unshod and the shod Carmelites—each would operate independently. Even though her health was failing, Teresa resumed her organizing, traveling by carriage over rough roads to administer the seven convents she had founded and to lay plans for others.

The gifts of God to Teresa were many. She was wise, yet practical; a mystic and yet an energetic reformer. She was a woman for God, a woman of prayer, discipline, and compassion. Her heart belonged to God. She was misunderstood, misjudged, opposed in her efforts at reform. Yet she struggled on, courageous and faithful. In the midst of her illness and opposition she clung to God in prayer and surrender.

Teresa was also a woman for others. Although she was a contemplative, she spent much of her time and energy seeking to reform herself and the Carmelites, to lead them back to the full observance of the primitive rule. In all the people she touched, she was a woman for the service of others, a woman who inspired.

Of her five books, the most widely read is *The Interior Castle*, her analogy of the soul's progress from self-knowledge into the presence of God. She wrote it for her nuns.

A Dedicated Life

Teresa spent her sixty-seven years to know God, and to know herself in relation to God. All self-knowledge, she taught, depends on recognition of the dignity and beauty of the soul created in God's image. For her the response of her soul to Christ was an arduous, mystical pilgrimage toward a poverty of spirit, a spiritual perfection. "Be patient," she advised the nuns in her care; "let grace be the guide through the rooms of the soul's interior castle. Be brave and dare with a holy boldness."

Teresa knew well the continued presence and value of suffering, such as physical illness, opposition to reform, and difficulties in prayer, but she grew to be able to embrace suffering and even desire it. She prayed: "Lord, either to suffer or to die. How true it is that whoever works for You is paid in troubles! And what a precious price to those who love You if we understand its value."

She left this advice to those who suffer, a poem found in her Office book after her death in 1582: "Be not perplexed, be not afraid, everything passes, God does not change. Patience wins all things. He who has God lacks nothing; God alone suffices."

Teresa was declared a saint in 1622, and in 1970 Pope Paul VI made her the first woman Doctor (distinguished teacher) of Catholicism.

The feast day of Saint Teresa of Jesus is October 15, on which the Church prays: "O God, who through your Spirit raised up Saint Teresa of Jesus to show the Church the way to seek perfection, grant that we may always be nourished by the food of her heavenly teaching and fired with longing for true holiness."

ROBERT BELLARMINE
(1542-1621)

ROBERT Bellarmine was born in 1542 in the town of Monte Pulciano in Tuscany. He began his novitiate in the Society of Jesus. Ill health was his cross all during his life.

After his ordination in 1570, he became the great defender of the Church against the followers of the Protestant Reformation. Lay people and clergy, Catholics and Protestants, read his volumes with eagerness. A promising scholar from his youth, he devoted his energy to the study of Church history and the Fathers of the Church, as well as Holy Scripture. He revised the Latin Bible.

Robert was made Rector of the Jesuit College, Provincial of his Order in Naples, and theologian to Pope Clement VIII. He wrote two famous catechisms. The Pope nominated him a cardinal because he said "he had not his equal for learning."

Having been appointed Archbishop of Capua, Robert laid aside his books and began preahing to the people, teaching catechism to the children, visiting the sick, and helping the poor. But three years later Pope Paul V insisted on having Cardinal Bellarmine at his side. From then on he was head of the Vatican Library. As a member of almost every Congregation at the Vatican, he took an important part in the affairs of the Holy See.

A Saintly Scholar

Bellarmine's most famous work is his three volume *Disputations on the Controversies of the Christian Faith.* Noteworthy are the sections on the temporal power of the Pope and the role of the laity.

While he occupied apartments in the Vatican, Bellarmine relaxed none of his former austerities. He limited his household expenses to what was barely essential, eating only the food available to the poor.

Robert Bellarmine devoted his life to the study of Scripture and Catholic doctrine. His writings help us understand that not only is the content of our faith important, it is the living person of Jesus—as revealed by His life, death and resurrection—that is the source of revelation. The real source of our faith is not merely a set of doctrines but rather the person of Christ still living in the Church today. When He left His Apostles, Jesus assured them of His living presence: "When the Spirit of truth comes, He will lead you to the complete truth." His words of farewell were: "Know that I am with you always, until the end of the world."

The Yoke of Christ

In his treatise *On the Ascent of the Mind to God,* Robert Bellarmine writes: " 'O Lord, You are gracious and full of mercy.' Who would refuse to serve You with all their hearts once they have begun to taste even slightly the delights of Your paternal authority? What, after all, do You ask of Your servants? 'Take My yoke upon you,' You declare. And what kind of yoke is it? You say, 'My yoke is easy and My burden is light.' Who then would be unwilling to bear a yoke that does not crush but rather encourages; a burden that does not weigh down but rather strengthens? Hence, You rightly added: 'And you will find rest for yourselves.'

"And what is this yoke that does not weary but actually gives rest? It is the first and the greatest of the commandments: 'You shall love the Lord, your God, with all your whole heart.' Can anything be easier, more delightful, or more agreeable than to love the goodness, beauty, and love that You constitute to perfection?

"Moreover, do You not also promise a reward to those who keep Your commandments—a reward that is 'more desirable than gold and sweeter than honey'? Indeed, You promise an infinite reward, as Saint James the Apostle declares: 'The Lord has prepared the crown of life for those He loves.' And what is this crown of life? A greater good than anything we can imagine or desire— this is how it is described by Saint Paul inspired by

Isaiah: 'Eye has not seen, nor has ear heard, nor has it entered into the heart of human beings what things God has prepared for those who love Him.' Truly, there is a great reward for keeping Your commandments."

Robert Bellarmine died at Rome in 1621 at the age of seventy-nine. His feast day is September 17, on which the Church prays: "O God, in order to vindicate Your faith, You endowed Saint Robert, Your Bishop, with wondrous erudition and virtues. Through his intercession, grant that Your people may ever rejoice in the integrity of his faith."

CAMILLUS OF LELLIS
(1550-1613)

C AMILLUS was born in Bocchianico, Italy, in 1550. His mother died when he was a child. His father neglected him, and he grew up with an excessive

love for gambling. He went with his father at the age of
seventeen to fight with the Venetians against the Turks,
who had conquered the last remnant of the old Christian
(Byzantine) Empire in the East. On the campaign he
contracted a leg infection that troubled him the rest of
his life.

About 1575 Camillus entered Saint James Hospital
for the incurably ill in Rome. He was both a patient and
a servant, as it was common for hospital nurses and or-
derlies to have no medical training. Surprisingly, his
health improved, but his rough, quarrelsome ways
bothered people, so he was dismissed to return to the
world.

Camillus was a huge man, reportedly six feet, six
inches tall, and a soldier-of-fortune in his youth. He succeeded in gambling away even the shirt off his back so
that he was destitute in Naples. He took a job as a day
laborer on a new building for a Capuchin community.
Under the guidance of friars, he was reintroduced to
Christianity. Prevented from entering a religious Order
because of his diseased leg, he returned to Rome and to
Saint James Hospital to work again as a servant.

Working with the Sick

In spite of the apparently incurable sore on his leg,
Camillus served the sick with great compassion. His dedication was rewarded by his being made superinten-
dent. Distressed by the uncaring attitudes of many hospital attendants, Camillus and a small group of other
serious-minded servants banded together to improve the
service.

With the advice of his friend Saint Philip Neri, he studied for the priesthood and was ordained at the age of 34. He and two companions left Saint James with the intention of establishing their own hospital. The community grew, developing as a kind of traveling medical corps pledged to care for sick prisoners, victims of plague, and any other ill people.

In 1591 Pope Gregory XIV recognized Camillus and his group as the Ministers of the Sick. As the badge of the Order, the founder chose a large red cross. During the last decade of the sixteenth century, Camillians formed the first field ambulance corps by rescuing the wounded from the battlefields in Hungary and Croatia.

Meanwhile, Camillus founded a second house in Naples, where the ministry included care for plague-stricken sailors. Two Camillians died in that labor, becoming the first recorded martyrs to Church-related public health service.

Camillus founded fifteen houses of his Order and eight hospitals. He labored hard to improve hospital and general medical practices.

Love for the Sick

One of his companions speaks of Camillus in these words: "I must begin with holy charity since it is the root of all virtues and Saint Camillus' most characteristic charism. I would therefore say that he was ablaze with the ardor of this virtue not only toward God but also toward his fellow human beings, especially the sick. So true was this that he merely had to see a sick person and his heart was overcome with compassion such as to make him forget entirely all earthly pleasures, delights, and attachments. Whenever he was caring for any sickness, he seemed to become totally immersed in and consumed by his great dedication. . . .

"Camillus saw the person of Christ in every sick person with such vividness of imagination that often in serving the sick their food he actually regarded them as being other Christs. . . . To imbue his religious with love for this primordial virtue, he was accustomed to repeating for them these most comforting words of Christ: 'I was sick and you visited Me.' Indeed, he pronounced these words so often that he seemed to have them engraved on his heart. So deep and so wide-ranging was the charity of Saint Camillus that he embraced in his goodness and benevolence not only the sick and the dying but in a general way all the poor and the suffering."

Tired and barely able to walk, the Camillian superior relinquished his leadership in 1607, but until his death six years later he continued to assist at the motherhouse in Rome. He died shortly after completing a visitation of all the Order's hospitals.

The feast of Saint Camillus is celebrated on July 18, when the Church prays: "O God, You adorned Saint Camillus, Your priest, with the singular grace of charity toward the sick. By his merits, pour fourth the spirit of Your love into us, so that by serving You in our brothers and sisters here on earth we may safely come to You at the hour of death."

JANE FRANCES DE CHANTAL
(1562-1641)

JANE Frances was born in Dijon, France, in 1562. She was the second child of the president of the French Parliament of Burgundy. At the age of twenty she married the Baron de Chantal, an officer in the army of Henry IV. Her husband was killed by accident while hunting and died in her arms. She was left a widow at the age of twenty-eight with one little son and three daughters, after seven years of marriage.

When she was thirty-two, she met Saint Francis de Sales, who became her spiritual director. She wanted to be a nun, but he persuaded her to defer this decision. She took a vow to remain unmarried and to obey her director.

Order of the Visitation

After three years Francis told her of his plan to found an institute of women which would be a haven for those whose health, age, or other considerations barred them from entering the already established Orders. There would be no cloister, and they would be free to undertake spiritual and corporal works of mercy. They were to exemplify the virtues of Mary at the Visitation.

With the help of Francis, Jane Frances laid the foundation of her new "Order of the Visitation of Our Lady" at Annecy in 1610 at the age of forty-five. The usual opposition arose and Francis de Sales was obliged to make it a cloistered community, with the Rule of Saint Augustine.

Jane Frances underwent great sufferings: Francis de Sales died, her son was killed, a plague ravaged France, and she had to endure great trials of the spirit—interior anguish, darkness, and spiritual dryness.

Saint Vincent de Paul said of her: "She was full of faith, and yet all her life long she had been tormented by thoughts against it. Nor did she once grow lax in the fidelity God asked of her. And so I regard her as one of the holiest souls I have ever met on this earth."

A Martyrdom of Love

One day Jane Frances spoke these words to her sisters, which were taken down exactly as spoken: "My dear daughters, many of our holy Fathers, pillars of the Church, did not suffer martyrdom. Why do you think this happened? I think it happened because there is another martydom, one termed the martyrdom of love. In this martyrdom, God sustains the lives of His servants so that they give themselves for His glory and makes them martyrs and confessors at the same time. I know that it is to this martyrdom that the Daughters of the Visitation are destined, and that God will bestow it on those who are so fortunate as to desire it.

"Give yourselves entirely to God, and you will experience this martyrdom. The Divine Love directs its sword at our innermost being and separates us from ourselves. I know one person whom love separated from all that was dearest to her as if a persecutor's sword had separated her body from her soul. . . .

"As far as I am concerned, the martyrdom of love is not on a lower level than the other martyrdom because 'love is as strong as death.' In keeping their lives to do God's will, martyrs of love experience sufferings that are a thousand times greater than the sufferings they would incur if they died a thousand times to bear witness to their faith, charity, and fidelity."

Jane Frances visited eighty-seven convents of the Order. She died December 13, 1641, at the age of sixty-nine. Her feast day is August 12, on which the Church prays: "O God, who made Saint Jane Frances de Chantal radiant with outstanding merits in different walks of life, grant us, through her intercession, that, walking faithfully in our vocation, we may constantly be examples of shining light."

FRANCIS DE SALES
(1567-1622)

FRANCIS was born at Savoy in 1567. At First Communion, he decided that he would be a priest, but his father decided otherwise: his son would study law and become a famous lawyer and a member of the senate of Savoy. So Francis went to Paris to begin his education, and after five years of that, in obedience to his father's wishes, he set off for Padua, at that time the site of one of the greatest law schools of Europe, to study Canon and Civil Law.

Francis was twenty-four when he left Padua, a Doctor of Law, and one of the most brilliant graduates of the university. When Francis returned home, his father

142

made life miserable for him, demanding that he marry and settle down, but Francis refused. Then something happened to change his father's mind. The head or Provost of the Cathedral Chapter of Geneva in Switzerland died, and the Pope appointed Francis in his place. This meant that he would have to be a priest. In December 1593, Francis de Sales was ordained a priest.

Religious Turmoil

At this time a whole section of Switzerland had been taken over by the Protestants. Besides this, part of the country to the south of Lake Constance had also been taken from Savoy, and the Catholic religion had been entirely wiped out. To this land Francis now offered to go as a missionary, to preach and work to restore the faith. For four years Francis and the others—for other priests soon joined him—worked, preaching, arguing, suffering, and half the time starving. The Protestants tried over and over to kill him but each time he escaped. Gradually, the Protestants began to come back to the Church and at the end of four years, there were 75,000 Catholics where before there had been only a hundred.

But now there was new work for him. The Bishop of Geneva was old and he wanted Francis to be made his helper and to succeed him when he died. So in 1599 Francis was consecrated coadjutor bishop. The Church had to be built up again: parishes and religious houses had to be established, the diocese had to be visited, and he had to make many of his journeys on foot. For twenty-three years he worked as bishop.

While administering his diocese Francis continued to preach, hear confessions, and catechize the children. His gentle character was a great asset in winning souls. He practiced his own slogan: "A spoonful of honey attracts more flies than a barrelful of vinegar."

Patron of the Catholic Press

In addition to his two well-known books, *The Introduction to the Devout Life* and *Treatise on the Love of God,* Francis wrote many pamphlets and carried on a vast correspondence. For his writings, he has been named patron of the Catholic Press. His writings, filled with his characteristic gentle spirit, are addressed to lay people. He wanted to make them understand that they too are called to be saints.

The saintly bishop stated: "At the time of creation, God commanded the plants to bring forth their fruits, each one according to its kind. In the same way, He commands all Christians—who are the living plants of His Church—to bring forth the fruits of devotion, according to the characteristics, state, and vocation of each. . . . True devotion not only does no injury to any vocation or employment but also adorns and beautifies it. . . . It is an error to say that devotion is incompatible with the life of a soldier, a businessman, a prince, or a married woman. . . . In whatever state we find ourselves, we can and should aspire to a perfect life."

Francis tells us: "Those who possess Christian meekness are affectionate and tender toward everyone. They are disposed to forgive and excuse the frailties of others. The goodness of their heart appears in a sweet affability that influences their words and actions, and presents every object to their view in the most charitable and pleasing light.''

In spite of his busy life, Francis had time to collaborate with Saint Jane Frances de Chantal, in the work of establishing the Sisters of the Visitation.

Francis died quietly, at the age of fifty-six, at Lyons on December 28, 1622. His feast is celebrated on January 24, on which the Church prays: "Father in heaven, You prompted Saint Francis de Sales to become all things to all for the salvation of all. May his example inspire us to dedicated love in the service of our brothers and sisters.''

ALOYSIUS GONZAGA
(1568-1591)

ALOYSIUS was born of the princely family of Castiglione in 1568 near Mantua in Lombardy. As a little boy he spent some time with his father in the army. As a son of a princely family, he grew up in royal courts and army camps. His father wanted him to be a military hero.

When he was thirteen, Aloysius traveled with his parents and the Empress of Austria to Spain and acted as a page in the court of Philip II in Madrid. The more he saw of court life, the more he sought relief in learning about the lives of the saints. His motto was: "I was born for greater things." A book about the experiences of Jesuit missionaries in India suggested to him the idea of entering the Society of Jesus. At twenty he signed away forever his right to the title and lands of the Gonzagas and became a Jesuit novice.

Aloysius spent four years in the study of philosophy and had Saint Robert Bellarmine as his spiritual adviser. He fasted, scourged himself, and sought solitude and prayer. But for his own good he was obliged to eat more and to take recreation with the othe students, and he was forbidden to pray except at stated times.

Love for His Mother

Aloysius loved his mother very much, for she was his first teacher in holiness. In a letter to her he wrote: "Most illustrious lady: I beg for you the perpetual grace and consolation of the Holy Spirit. When your letter arrived, I was in this region of the dying. But now for some time I have an aspiration toward heaven so that we may praise the eternal God in the land of the living. Indeed, I was hoping to have completed this journey even before now.

"It is charity, as Saint Paul says, 'to weep with those who weep and to rejoice with those who rejoice.'

Then, my illustrious mother, you must surely derive joy from the fact that by reason of your favor and generosity, God has pointed out true joy to me and given me the security of never losing Him. . . .

"God summons me to an eternal rest in recompense for such a brief and slight labor. He calls me from heaven to the supreme happiness which I have sought with such carelessness and promises the reward for the tears I have so infrequently shed. . . . This will not be a perpetual separation; we shall see each other again in heaven where we shall be joined with our Savior. We shall praise Him with all the powers of our soul, sing His mercies forever, and enjoy unending bliss.

"God only takes from us now what He had loaned us previously with no other purpose but to keep it in a surer and safer place, and He will furnish us with those joys that we would desire for ourselves. . . . I have willingly written these things because there is nothing more that I could do to show the love and reverence I owe you as a son to his mother."

Victim of the Plague

In 1561, a plague struck Rome. The Jesuits opened a hospital of their own where they rendered personal service. Because he nursed patients, washing them and making their beds, Aloysius caught the disease himself. A fever persisted after recovery and he was so weak he could scarcely rise from bed. Yet, he maintained his great discipline of prayer, knowing that he would die within the octave of Corpus Christi.

Three months later, on June 21, 1591, Aloysius passed away quietly as he gazed at a crucifix where he found strength to suffer. He was only twenty-three years old. He never reached the priesthood.

His feast day is celebrated on June 21, on which the Church prays: "O God, author of all heavenly gifts, You gave Saint Aloysius both a wonderful innocence of life and a deep spirit of penance. Through his merits grant that we may imitate his penitence."

MARTIN DE PORRES
(1579-1639)

MARTIN de Porres was born at Lima in Peru of a Spanish father and a black mother in 1579. He grew up in poverty and had a deep understanding and love for the poor. When quite young, he went to work for a surgeon where he learned about medicine and how to care for the sick and and the wounded.

After a few years in this medical apostolate, he applied to the Dominicans to be a "lay helper," not feeling himself worthy to be a religious brother. After nine years, the example of his prayer and penance, charity and humility led the community in 1603 to request him to make full religious profession. With joy and generosity he performed lowly tasks in the kitchen, laundry, wardrobe room, and infirmary. Many of his nights were spent in prayer and penitential practices; his days were filled with nursing the sick and caring for the poor.

Martin was instrumental in founding an orphanage, took care of slaves brought from Africa, and managed the daily alms of the priory. He became a fund-raiser, obtaining thousands of dollars for poor girls, so that they could marry or enter a convent. He was a good friend of another Dominican saint of Peru, Rose of Lima.

Love for All God's Creatures

Brother Martin was always very cheerful and very simple. He loved God with a great love. He also loved all human beings as well as all creatures very much, because God had made them all. There is a story that one day he found some mice among the clothing in the sacristy. Taking one of them in his hands, he said: "My little brother mouse, I don't know whether you are the guilty one for all the damage done in the sacristy and in the wardrobe. But today you and your friends will have to leave the monastery."

Later all the mice gathered around the saint, and he placed them in a basket. He brought them to an open field and let them loose. He brought them food. Indeed, so great was Martin's love for animals that he set up and maintained a hospital for dogs and cats at the home of his sister Juana.

Martin had unbounded love for Jesus in the Blessed Sacrament. Holy Mass was the center of his daily life. Holy Communion was his way of loving Jesus and of making his soul holy. Free hours would be spent before the tabernacle. He was also devoted to Mary, the Immaculate Mother of Our Savior.

Blessed with the gift of healing, Martin once cured the ailing Archbishop of Mexico with a touch of his hand. God chose to fill Martin's life with extraordinary gifts.

A Shining Example for All Christians

Martin died of a fever in 1639, and was beatified in 1873. On May 6, 1962, he was canonized by Pope John XXIII. On that occasion, Pope John said: "Saint Martin, ever obedient to his Divine Master, treated his brothers and sisters with the greatest love born of solidity of faith and simplicity of heart. He loved others because he sincerely regarded them as children of God and his own brothers and sisters. Indeed, he loved them even more than himself, because his humility led him to regard all others as more upright and better than himself.

"Martin excused the failings of others and pardoned their most grievous offenses, since he was convinced that he deserved far greater punishment on account of the sins he had committed. With unflagging zeal he strove to set the wicked on the right path again and cared for the sick with true kindness. He obtained food and clothing for the poor and rendered all the assistance he could to farm-laborers, blacks, and mulattos, who were denigrated as the lowest of slaves. All this earned for him the title 'Martin the Charitable.' . . .

"May the example of Saint Martin teach all those striving for salvation what delights and what happiness they can find in following in the footsteps of Jesus Christ and obeying His commandments."

The feast day of Martin de Porres is November 3, on which the Church prays: "O God, You led Saint Martin by the way of humility to heavenly glory. Help us to follow his holiness and so become worthy to be exalted with him in heaven."

ROSE OF LIMA
(1586-1617)

ROSE de Flores was born in Lima in 1586 and received the name Isabel at her baptism. She was called Rose for her beauty. She came into the world at a time when South America was in its first century of evangelization, fifty years after the Spanish completed their conquest of Peru's Incan people. Her father was Spanish; some accounts say her mother was Incan.

Rose objected as a child to any mention of her physical beauty because she found praise an obstacle to humility. She is said to have rubbed her face with pepper to produce disfiguring blotches. As a young woman Rose wished to enter a convent, but was prevented by her family. She refused to marry. When her father suffered a financial loss in a mining venture, she took up needlework to help the family.

Out of obedience Rose continued her life of penance and solitude at home, as a member of the Third Order of Saint Dominic. Catherine of Siena seems to have been Rose's model. She lived in a small enclosure in the garden. She did handwork, tended the flowers, prayed, and kept up her guard against evil invading her heart.

Beginning of Social Services

Rose emerged from seclusion around 1614. She lived her remaining three years in the home of a government official. During this time she set up a room in the house, where she cared for homeless children, the elderly, and the sick. This was the beginning of social services in Peru.

Rose wrote: "The Lord our Savior lifted up His voice and said with unparalleled majesty: 'All must understand that grace comes only after tribulation. They must realize that without the weight of afflictions they cannot reach the heights of grace. . . . Without the cross they cannot find the path to attain heaven.'. . . A powerful impulse then took hold of me and impelled me to preach the beauty of Divine grace. . . .

"If only human beings could realize the importance of Divine grace and how beautiful, noble, and precious it really is! How many riches it contains and how many treasures of gladness and delight! . . . This is the reward and the ultimate fruit of patience. No person would ever complain about the cross or the punishments that may come, if they knew the scales on which these are weighed for their distribution to human beings."

Rose also pointed strongly toward the Cross as the source of purity. Her spirituality shows how she wanted and worked for inner purity. Her single desire was to banish self-love from her heart that it might be filled with the love of Christ. She had so great a love of God that what indeed sometimes seemed imprudent was simply a logical carrying out of a conviction that anything that might endanger a loving relationship with God must be rooted out.

Rose's spirituality, her obsession with purity of heart, seems strange to many in our day unless it is read in terms of Saint Paul's observation, "God chose the world's lowborn and despised, those who count for nothing, to reduce to nothing those who were something; so that mankind can do no boasting before God. God it is who has given you life in Christ Jesus." (1 Cor 1:28-30)

The First Saint of the Americas

What might have been a merely eccentric life was transfigured from the inside. We should remember the greatest thing about Rose: a love of God so ardent that it withstood ridicule from without, violent temptation, and lengthy periods of sickness. At her death in 1617 at the age of thirty-one, the city of Lima gave her a heroine's funeral. Prominent men took turns carrying her coffin.

Rose is the first saint of the Americas. Her feast day is celebrated on August 23, on which the Church prays: "O God, You filled Saint Rose with love for You and enabled her to leave the world and be free for You through the austerity of penance. Through her intercession, help us to follow in her footsteps on earth and enjoy the torrent of Your delights in heaven.''

MARGARET MARY ALACOQUE
(1647-1690)

MARGARET Mary was born in 1647, the fifth of seven children, in the diocese of Autún in France. She was physically handicapped, but the Blessed Virgin cured her. In thanksgiving she promised to give her life to God.

Her early years were marked by sickness and a painful home situation. ''The heaviest of my crosses was that I could do nothing to lighten the cross my mother was suffering.''

When she was seventeen, Jesus appeared to her, just as He was after He was scourged. She decided at once to enter the Order of Visitation nuns at Paray-le-Monial at the age of twenty-four.

A fellow novice termed Margaret humble, simple and frank, but above all kind and patient under sharp criticism and correction. She could not meditate in the formal way expected, though she tried her best to give up her "prayer of simplicity." Slow and quiet, she was assigned to help an infirmarian who was very energetic.

Revelations to Margaret

On December 27, 1674, when Margaret was three years a nun, she received the first of her revelations. The request of Christ was that His love for mankind be made evident through her. During the next 13 months, He appeared to her at intervals. His human heart was to be the symbol of His divine-human love. By her own love she was to make up for the coldness and ingratitude of the world—by frequent and loving Holy Communion, especially on the first Friday of each month, and by an hour's vigil of prayer every Thursday night in memory of His agony and isolation in Gethsemane. He also asked that a feast of reparation be instituted.

Jesus made at least twelve promises to Margaret. Some of those promises are: that He would bless those who honor His Sacred Heart, that He would give them all the graces they need, that He would give them sufficient graces to die in the state of grace if they received Communion on nine First Fridays in succession.

Jesus said to her: "Look at this Heart which has loved human beings so much, and yet men do not want to love Me in return. Through you My divine Heart wishes to spread its love everywhere on earth."

Like all saints, Margaret had to pay for her gift of holiness. Some of her own sisters were hostile. Some theologians called her visions delusions. Parents of children she taught called her an imposter and innovator. A new confessor, Blessed Claude de la Columbière, a Jesuit, recognized her genuineness and supported her.

The Sacred Heart—An Inexhaustible Fountain

Concerning the Sacred Heart of Jesus, she wrote: "It seems to me that the purpose of Our Lord's great desire that His Sacred Heart be honored by some particular homage is to renew in our souls the effects of the Redemption. For His Sacred Heart is a never-ending source that seeks to be poured out in hearts that are humble, open, and completely unattached so as to prepare them to offer themselves to His good pleasure.

"This Divine Heart is an inexhaustible source that gives rise to three continuously flowing streams. The first is the stream of mercy for sinners, which dispenses on us the spirit of contrition and repentance. The second is the stream of charity, which dispenses help on all who are afflicted and in need, especially those tending to perfection who will find therein the means to overcome obstacles. The third stream dispenses love and light on His perfect friends whom He wishes to unite with Himself, so that they may share His knowledge and His maxims and dedicate themselves entirely to obtaining His glory in their own individual way."

After serving as novice mistress and assistant superior, Margaret died while being anointed at the age of 43, in the year 1690.

Her spirituality can be summarized in her words: "I need nothing but God and to lose myself in the Heart of Jesus."

Her feast day is celebrated on October 16, on which the Church prays: "O Lord, pour out upon us the spirit with which You enriched Saint Margaret Mary. Help us to know the love of Christ which is too great for human knowledge and to be filled with the fullness of God."

ALPHONSUS LIGUORI
(1696-1787)

ALPHONSUS Liguori was born at Marianella, near Naples, September 27, 1696. His father was Joseph Liguori, a naval officer and Captain of the Royal

Galleys, a man of genuine faith. His mother was Donna Anna Cavalieri, of Spanish descent. She was an inspiration for her son.

Alphonsus started out in life as a lawyer. At the age of sixteen he was made a doctor of law. In the eight years of practice he never lost a case. Though he was renowned as a doctor of both Canon and Civil Law, he left the legal profession and entered the priesthood on November 21, 1726. For six years he labored in and around Naples preaching missions. He had a burning zeal for souls and devoted himself to the most neglected. To carry on this work he founded the Congregation of the Most Holy Redeemer at Scala. The rule of the Redemptorists was approved by Benedict XIV in 1748. Today they number more than six thousand and are spread throughout the whole world. Their founder wished them to preach practical sermons, retreats, and missions.

In the guidance of souls, Alphonsus was always kind and sympathetic. His confessional was usually crowded, and hardened sinners returned to the healing sacrament in great numbers.

An Active Life

At the age of sixty-six Alphonsus was prevailed upon to become the Bishop of Saint Agatha, and he undertook the reform of his diocese. He sent out a band of priests to conduct a general mission throughout the diocese of 30,000 souls.

He wrote and published about sixty books on the spiritual life, morals, and dogma. Many of these books were written in the half hours snatched from his labors as a missionary, religious superior, and bishop, or in continual bodily and mental suffering.

In a sermon Alphonsus wrote: "All of the soul's sanctity and perfection consists in love for Jesus Christ, our God, our Supreme Good, and our Redeemer. It is this love which gathers together and safeguards all the virtues that make a person perfect. Does God not deserve all our love? He Himself has loved us from all eternity! . . .

"To obtain our love, the eternal Father went so far as to give all of Himself to us. He went so far as to give His only Son for us. What did He do when He saw that we were dead in sin and deprived of His grace? Moved by His immense love for us—or rather as the Apostle says, 'because of His superabundant love' for us—He sent His beloved Son to make satisfaction for us and to summon us back to the life that we had lost through sin. But by giving us the Son whom He chastised so that He might spare us, He also gave every good: grace, love, and paradise; for all these goods are obviously inferior to His Son."

Persecutions

Alphonsus met with many persecutions and disappointments till his death. Though he was a very old man and had lived a life of heroic sanctity, he had to suffer many terrible temptations against faith and virtue.

In June 1767, Alphonsus was attacked by terrible rheumatic pains which developed into an illness from which he was never to recover. He was left with a permanent and incurable bending of the neck, familiar from the portraits of him. Arthritis had gripped his wrists.

They were swollen and so sore that he could not endure even the touch of the sheets against them. Later the inflamation spread to all his other joints. The least movement caused him pain. Yet he continued handling details of work from his bed.

Alphonsus died on August 1, 1787. He was canonized in 1839 and was declared a Doctor of the Church in 1871.

Alphonsus is best known for his moral theology, but he also wrote well in the field of spiritual and dogmatic theology. His *Glories of Mary* is one of the great works on that subject, and his book *Visits to the Blessed Sacrament* went through forty editions in his lifetime, greatly influencing the practice of this devotion in the Church.

His feast is celebrated on August 1, on which the Church prays: "O God, You constantly introduce new examples of virtue in Your Church. Walking in the footsteps of Saint Alphonsus, Your bishop, may we be consumed with zeal for souls and attain the rewards he has won in heaven."

ELIZABETH BAYLEY SETON
(1774-1821)

ELIZABETH Ann Bayley Seton was born in New York City August 28, 1774, a true daughter of the American Revolution, just two years before the Declaration of Independence. She was the daughter of a surgeon and a frail mother who died when she was three years old. She and a sister were raised partly by relatives. By birth and marriage, she was linked to the first families of New York and enjoyed the fruits of high society. Reared a staunch Episcopalian by her mother and stepmother, she learned the value of prayer, Scripture and nightly examination of conscience. Her father, Dr. Richard Bayley, did not have much use for Churches but was a great humanitarian, teaching his daughter to love and serve others.

Elizabeth Bayley and William Magee Seton, a member of an illustrious mercantile family, married in 1794. They lived for a time at 27 Wall Street, then a fashionable residential address, and summered in the village of Bloomingdale, located where 79th Street now crosses Manhattan Island. They had five children.

A New Home

Elizabeth Seton might well have spent her whole life as a contented New York matron, active in Trinity Episcopal Church, had it not been for her husband's health. He probably had tuberculosis. His physical condition worsened, and so did the family business. In 1803, Elizabeth, William, and their oldest child, Anna, set sail for Italy, where they had business associates, to find a healthier climate for Mr. Seton. He died before the year's end.

Widow and child stayed in Italy for several months. Her serious introduction to Catholicism is believed to have come in Italy, especially through the members of the Filicchi family. Once home, Mrs. Seton was hard pressed to support herself, three daughters, and two sons. She was religiously pushed and pulled from one side by Protestant friends and from the other primarily by Antonio Filicchi, who was in America on business.

Conversion

While in Italy with her dying husband, Elizabeth witnessed Catholicity in action through family friends. Many of her friends and relatives rejected her when she became a Catholic in March 1805. These basic points led her to become Catholic: belief in the Real Presence of Christ in the Eucharist, devotion to the Blessed Virgin Mary, and conviction that the Catholic Church led back to the Apostles and to Christ. She wrote: "How often I argued to my fearful uncertain heart: at all events Catholics must be as safe as any other religion. They say none are safe but themselves—perhaps it is true. If not, at all events I shall be as safe with them as any."

To pay the bills, she tried running a boarding house. She failed. She failed also in a private school she opened with friends. A priest suggested Maryland, a state founded by Catholics, as a place for her to begin an American teaching sisterhood. In 1809, she relocated adjacent to Saint Mary's Seminary in Baltimore, and there began what would become the American branch of the Sisters of Charity of Saint Vincent de Paul.

Sisters of Charity

The next year Mrs. Seton and a small community of women, including her daughters (the sons were in boarding school), moved to Emmitsburg. Her idea was to establish a free, coeducational school for poor rural children, but funds were too limited. To survive financially, paying students—girls—from cities were needed. The school had some local and some poor children; its chief support came with the daughters of rich families in New York, Philadelphia, and Baltimore. She remarked that her hope of "a nursery only for Our Savior's poor country children" had given way to a school "forming city girls to faith and piety as wives and mothers."

Teachers at the school at Emmitsburg were well trained and supervised. Rich or poor, children were drawn to Mother Seton as much as she was drawn to them. Her gift for mothering extended individually to the girls, and also to the boys at the nearby Mount Saint Mary's School.

The early years at Emmitsburg were difficult. The sisterhood, first called the Society of Saint Joseph, had trouble finding its direction. Mother Seton's position as superior was not secure until 1816, and her work was interrupted in 1812 and again in 1816 by the deaths of her oldest and youngest daughters. Mother Seton had able assistance from her nuns in expanding beyond Emmitsburg, first to an orphanage in Philadelphia, and before her death to another in New York and to schools in those cities. The American Sisters of Charity had some fifty members in 1821, a good number considering that the Catholic population of the United States was only 200,000 out of 7.2 million people.

Spiritual Development

The thousand or more letters of Mother Seton reveal the development of her spiritual life from ordinary goodness to heroic sanctity. She suffered great trials of sickness, misunderstanding, the death of loved ones (her husband and two young daughters) and the heartache of two sons. Neither William nor Richard was interested in religion, and the youngest failed in business.

In a conference to her spiritual daughters she wrote: "I will tell you what is my own great help. I once read or heard that an interior life means but the continuation of Our Savior's life in us; that the great object of all His mysteries is to merit for us the grace of His interior life and communicate it to us, it being the end of His mission to lead us into the sweet land of promise, a life of constant union with Himself. And what was the first rule of Our dear Savior's life? You know it was to do His Father's will.

"Well, then, the first end I propose in our daily work is to do the will of God; secondly, to do it in the manner He wills; and thirdly, to do it because it is His will. You are children of eternity. Your immortal crown awaits you, and the best of Fathers waits there to reward your duty and love. You may indeed sow here in tears, but you may be sure there to reap in joy."

In the decades following their founder's death at Emmitsburg, January 4, 1821, the Sisters of Charity became a major force in organizing schools, orphanages, hospitals, and colleges serving the whole of American society.

First American-Born Saint

Mother Seton is one of the keystones of the American Catholic Church. She founded the first native American religious community for women, the Sisters of Charity, opened the first American parish school and established the first American Catholic orphanage. All this she did in the span of 46 years while raising her five children.

She had two great devotions: abandonment to the will of God and an ardent love for the Blessed Sacrament. She wrote to a friend that she would prefer to exchange the world for a "cave or a desert. But God has given me a great deal to do, and I have always and hope always to prefer His will to every wish of my own." Her kind of sanctity is open to all if we love God and do His will.

On March 17, 1963, Pope John XXIII proclaimed her the first American-born citizen to be beatified. She was canonized by Pope Paul VI on September 14, 1975. Her feast day is January 4, on which the Church prays: "O God, who crowned with the gift of true faith Saint Elizabeth Ann Seton's burning zeal to find you, grant by her intercession and example that we may always seek you with diligent love and find you in daily service with sincere faith."

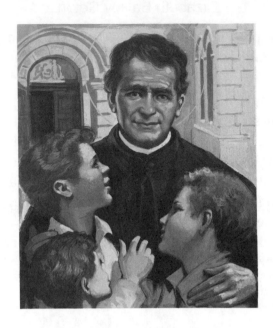

JOHN BOSCO
(1815-1888)

JOHN Bosco was born near Castelnuovo in the diocese of Turin, Italy, in 1815. His parents lived on a farm and were very poor. His father died when John was only two. One special virtue his mother taught her three boys was a love for poverty. As a youth John tended sheep.

Encouraged during his youth to become a priest so he would work with young boys, John was ordained in 1841. Several positions were offered but he felt that being an ordinary parish priest or teaching was not for him. He still wanted to do something for the boys he saw running about the streets of the city—orphans, thieves because they had to steal to live, boys who were trouble-some to the city and to themselves but who, John knew, wanted to be good citizens. And so it was that he offered to help a boy who could not serve his Mass.

The lad came back that night, and came again the next week bringing some of his pals with him. At first they could not quite figure out this big, smiling priest, who taught them religion, told them stories and did tricks to amuse them, and did not seem to care how much noise they made as long as they were decent. But it was not long before every spare minute Don Bosco had was taken up with the gangs of boys who sought him out. He named his work his Oratory of Saint Francis de Sales.

The Oratory

There were other people who objected to the goings on of Father Bosco and his gang. He was forced to hold his gatherings in the open fields and take his flock of boys—sometimes more than a hundred—to assist at Mass in whatever church they could get into.

Within a year Don Bosco had his boys under a roof, and as people realized what he was doing for the boys and for the whole city, they began to help. His one house or Oratory, as it was called, grew in a few years to four in the city of Turin. Each was filled to overflowing with boys whom he was educating not only in their faith but in general knowledge and in the trades. His boys were going out into all walks of life and making good. To all of them Don Bosco was their hero, and next to him was his mother, whom they fondly called Mamma Margaret, who had come to help with the boys, to cook and sew and mother them.

The Founding of the Salesians

Out of this beginning John Bosco founded a religious Order in 1859 to carry on his work and establish oratories in other cities—the Society of Saint Francis de Sales, or Salesians as they are better known. Their activity concentrated on education and mission work. Later, he organized a group of Salesian Sisters to assist girls.

John Bosco educated the whole person—body and soul united. He believed that Christ's love and our faith in that love should pervade everything we do—work, study, play. Yet John realized the importance of job-training and the self-esteem that comes with talent and ability so he trained his students in the trade crafts, too.

In a letter, John wrote: "If we wish to show ourselves as the friends of the true good of our students and oblige them to carry out their responsibilities, it is important above all never to forget that you represent the parents of these dear youths. It is these youths who have been the tender object of my concerns, studies, and priestly ministry, and that of our Salesian Congregation. . . .

"Let us regard as our children those over whom we must exercise some authority. Let us place ourselves always at their service, like Jesus who came to obey not to rule. Let us abhor anything that might give us the appearance of lording it over them. Let us dominate them only by serving them with greater pleasure. This is how Jesus dealt with His Apostles."

On January 31, 1888, John Bosco died. His work is being carried on today in many countries. He was declared a saint by Pope Pius XI in 1934, who himself had been acquainted with him. His feast is celebrated on January 31 on which the Church prays: "God of mercy, You called Saint John Bosco to be a father and teacher of the young. Grant that inspired by his ardent charity we may serve You alone and never tire of bringing others to Your Kingdom."

JOHN NEUMANN
(1811-1860)

JOHN Neumann was born on March 20, 1811 in what is now Czechoslovakia. After studying in Prague, he came to New York at twenty-five as a cleric and was then ordained in New York by Bishop Dubois. In 1840, he entered the Congregation of the Most Holy Redeemer (Redemptorists) and, at age twenty-nine, became the first of this Order to profess vows in the United States. He continued missionary work in Maryland, Virginia, Pennsylvania, and Ohio, where he became popular with the Germans. In 1852, at the age of 41, he was ordained Bishop of Philadelphia. There he worked hard for the establishment of parish schools and for the erection of many parishes for the numerous immigrants. The number of pupils in the parochial schools increased almost twentyfold within a short time. Gifted with outstanding organizing ability, he drew into the diocese many teaching Orders of Sisters and the Christian Brothers. During his brief assignment as Vice Provincial for the Redemptorists, he placed them in the forefront of the school system. He wrote a catechism which was widely used. While he was Bishop of Philadelphia more than 80 churches were built.

A Man of Many Talents

John knew eight Slavic dialects and modern languages. He traveled through his vast diocese by canal boat, stagecoach, railway, and on foot in his quest for souls.

John was well-known for his holiness and learning, spiritual writing and preaching.

When there was a question of dividing the diocese, Bishop Neumann expressed his willingness to resign. He wrote in a letter: "I was not a little disturbed by the fear that I had done something that so displeased the Holy Father that my resignation would appear desirable to his. If this be the case, I am prepared without any hesitation to leave the episcopacy. I have taken this burden out of obedience, and I have labored with all my powers to fulfill the duties of my office, and with God's help, as I hope, not without fruit.

"Indeed, I am much more accustomed to the country, and will be able to care for the people and faithful living in the mountains, in the coal mines, and on the farms, since I would be among them. I am ready to go where I may more securely prepare myself for death and for the account which must be rendered to the Divine Justice. I desire nothing but to fulfill the wish of the Holy Father whatever it may be."

First American Bishop-Saint

Bishop Neumann took seriusly Our Lord's words, "Go and teach all nations." From Christ he received his instructions and the power to carry them out. For Christ does not give a mission without supplying the means to accomplish it. The Father's gift in Christ to John Neumann was his exceptional organizing ability which he used to spread the Gospel and, above all, his example of simple faith and burning zeal for souls.

He died in 1860 performing his duties. On October 13, 1963, he became the first American bishop to be beatified. He was canonized on July 19, 1977.

His feast day is celebrated on January 5, on which day the Church prays: "O God, Light and Shepherd of souls, You established Saint John as bishop in Your Church to feed Your flock by his word and form it by his example. Help us through his intercession to keep the faith he taught by his word and follow the way he showed us by his example."

PIUS X
(1835-1914)

JOSEPH Sarto was the son of a poor village shoemaker and the oldest of ten children. He was born in 1835 in the village of Riese in the province of Venice. Two priests of the parish helped him through school because he wanted to become a priest. He went to the Padua seminary. After ordination he was made as assistant to the pastor in a small Italian town in the mountains. All the people loved him because he was kind and prayerful. They sensed his great love for God.

When he became Bishop of Mantua, he said, "I shall spare myself neither care nor labor nor earnest prayers for the salvation of souls. My hope is in Christ."

Bishop Sarto was made a cardinal, and, when Pope
Leo XIII died in 1903, he was elected Pope. His motto
was: "To restore all things in Christ, so that Christ may
be all in all." His constant teaching was: "Love God,
and lead good Christian lives." He wanted this to come
about through frequent Holy Communion. He is perhaps
best remembered for his encouragement of the frequent
reception of Holy Communion, especially by children.

Frequent Communion

In 1905, in his "Decree on Frequent Communion,"
Pope Pius X stated: "Frequent and daily Communion,
being most earnestly desired by Christ our Lord and by
the Catholic Church, should be open to all the faithful,
of whatever rank or condition of life. No one who is in
the state of grace, and who approaches the Holy Table
with an upright and devout intention, can be lawfully
hindered.

"At every Mass the faithful who are present snould
receive Communion, not only spiritually, by way of in-
ternal affection, but sacramentally, by the actual reception of the Eucharist."

On May 29, 1954, the day of the canonization of
Pope Pius X, Pope Pius XII said: "The Holy Eucharist
and the interior life: this is the supreme and universal
lesson which Pius X, from the height of glory, teaches in
this hour to all souls. As apostle of the interior life, he
becomes, in the age of the machine and organization,
the Saint and guide of men of our time.

"A priest, above all in the Eucharistic ministry: this
is the most faithful portrayal of Saint Pius X. From the
day of his sacred ordination until his death as Pope, he

knew no other path than this in order to arrive at heroism in his love of God and to bring about a wholehearted return to that Redeemer of the world, who by means of the Blessed Eucharist poured out the wealth of His divine love on men.''

Love for Scripture and the Liturgy

Pope Pius X expressed his love for Holy Scripture and the liturgy in his apostolic constitution: "Who can remain unmoved on hearing those numberless Psalms which in sublime fashion proclaim the majesty of God, His omnipotence, His ineffable justice, His goodness, His mercy, and His other infinite perfections? Who is not similarly inspired by the songs of thanksgiving for blessings received, by the humble and trusting prayers for additional favors as well as by the heartfelt prayers for pardon? . . .

"Who can remain without love for the One who is so faithfully prefigured by the Prophet David that is, Christ our Redeemer?"

His humble background was no obstacle in relating to a personal God and to people he loved genuinely. He said, "I was born poor, I lived poor, I will die poor." He gained his strength, his gentleness and warmth for people from the source of all gifts, the Spirit of Jesus. He was a man of God who knew the unhappiness of the world and the hardship of life, and in the greatness of his heart wanted to comfort everyone.

On the 11th anniversary of Pius X's election as Pope, Europe was plunged into World War I. He said, "This is the last affliction the Lord will visit on me. I would gladly give my life to save my poor children from this ghastly scourge." He died a few weeks after the war began, August 20, 1914 with the words, "To renew all things in Christ."

His feast is celebrated on August 21, when the Church prays: "O God, to preserve the Catholic Faith and renew all things in Christ, You filled Pope Saint Pius with heavenly wisdom and apostolic fortitude. Grant that we may follow his direction and example and be rewarded with eternal life with You."

MARIE BERNADETTE SOUBIROUS
(1844-1879)

BERNADETTE Soubirous was born on January 7, 1844 near Lourdes, in France. Her parents were very poor. Her father was a miller. He lost the mill and had to do odd jobs around town while his wife worked in the fields. At this time Bernadette was five years old, and already looked after the house and cared for her younger brothers and sisters. The family was forced to move to a rent-free room of a dilapidated building which once had been a town jail.

It was here that Bernadette contracted asthma in the damp atmosphere of the cell in Lourdes, so she was often sent to stay with friends, the Aravants, in the town of Bartres. There she helped with the housework and tended the sheep in the pasture. In return she received her board and lodging. In the evenings Madame Aravant taught her the catechism, the only education she ever received.

The Apparition of Mary Immaculate

In 1858 the Virgin Mary Immaculate appeared to Bernadette within the cave of Massabielle near Lourdes. Later, as a nun, she wrote a letter describing the experience. "I had gone down one day with two other girls to the bank of the river Gave when suddenly I heard a kind of rustling sound. I turned my heard toward the field by the side of the river but the trees seemed quite still and the noise was evidently not from there. Then I looked up and caught sight of the cave where I saw a lady wearing a lovely white dress with a bright belt. On top of each of her feet was a pale yellow rose, the same color as her rosary beads.

"At this I rubbed my eyes, thinking I was seeing things, and I put my hands into the fold of my dress where my Rosary was. I wanted to make the Sign of the Cross but for the life of me I couldn't manage it and my hand just fell down. Then the lady made the Sign of the Cross herself and at the second attempt I managed to do the same, though my hands were trembling. Then I began to say the Rosary while the lady let her beads slip through her fingers, without moving her lips. When I stopped saying the Hail Mary, she immediately vanished.

"I asked my two companions if they had noticed anything, but they said no. Of course they wanted to know what I was doing and I told them that I had seen a lady wearing a nice white dress, though I didn't know who she was. I told them not to say anything about it, and they said I was silly to have anything to do with it. I said they were wrong and I came back next Sunday, feeling myself drawn to the place. . . .

The Lady's Requests

"The third time I went the lady spoke to me and asked me to come every day for fifteen days. I said I would and then she said that she wanted me to tell the priests to build a chapel there. She also told me to drink from the stream. I went to the Gave, the only stream I could see. Then she made me realize she was not speaking of the Gave and she indicated a little trickle of water close-by. When I got to it I could only find a few drops of water but only at the fourth attempt was there sufficient for any kind of drink. The lady then vanished and I went back home.

"I went back each day for fifteen days and each time, except one Monday and one Friday, the lady appeared and told me to look for a stream and wash in it and to see that the priests built a chapel there. I must also pray, she said, for the conversion of sinners. I asked her many times what she meant by that, but she only smiled. Finally with outstretched arms and eyes looking up to heaven she told me she was the Immaculate Conception.

"During the fifteen days she told me three secrets but I was not to speak about them to anyone and so far have not."

Bernadette died, worn out with physical suffering, on April 16, 1879, at the age of thirty-six. Now her incorrupt body can be seen as she lay in death in the side chapel of the motherhouse of the Sisters of Charity at Nevers, where she lived and died as Sister Marie Bernard. Thirty years after her death her body was found in a perfect state of preservation—undoubtedly a token of love of the Immaculate Virgin Mary. She was beatified in 1925, and on December 8, 1933, she was canonized by Pope Pius XI.

Her feast day is April 16, on which day the Church prays: "God, protector and lover of the humble, You bestowed upon Your servant, Saint Bernadette, the favor of beholding the Immaculate Virgin Mary and of talking with her. Grant that we may deserve to behold You in heaven."

FRANCES XAVIER CABRINI

(1850-1917)

F RANCES Xavier Cabrini was born in Lombardy, Italy, in 1850, one of thirteen children. When she was eighteen years old, poor health kept her from entering religious life. She helped her mother and father until their death, and then worked on a farm with her brother and sister.

A priest asked her to teach in a girls' school. She stayed there for six years. Refused admission to the religious Order which had educated her to be a teacher, she began charitable work at the House of Providence Orphange in Cadogno, Italy. In September 1877 she made her vows there and took the religious habit.

When the bishop of the diocese of Lodi closed the orphanage in 1880, he named Frances prioress of the Missionary Sisters of the Sacred Heart. Seven young women from the orphanage joined with her to help poor children in hospitals and schools.

Since her early childhood, Frances had wanted to be a missionary in China. She wrote to Pope Leo XIII who told her, "Go to the United States, my child. There is much work awaiting you there."

Missionary in the United States

She came to the United States with six Sisters in 1889. She found disappointment and difficulties with every step. When she arrived in New York City, the house that was to be her first orphanage in the United States was not available. The archbishop advised her to return to Italy. But Frances left the archbishop's residence all the more determined to establish the orphanage. And she succeeded. She began working among the Italian people of New York and became an American citizen.

In thirty-five years Frances Xavier Cabrini founded sixty-seven institutions dedicated to caring for the poor, the abandoned, the uneducated and the sick. Seeing great need among Italian immigrants who were losing their faith, she organized schools and adult education classes. As a child, she was unable to overcome her fear of water, yet despite this fear, she traveled across the seas more than thirty times.

Her missionary zeal also led her to Central and South America where she founded schools in Argentina, Brazil, and Nicaragua.

Laboring for God's Glory

After twenty-eight years of missionary work she died of malaria in her own Columbus Hospital in Chicago on December 22, 1917. On July 7, 1946, she became the first United States citizen to be canonized. On that occasion Pope Pius XII said: "Although her constitution was very frail, her spirit was endowed with such singular strength that, knowing the will of God in her regard, she permitted nothing to impede her from accomplishing what seemed beyond the strength of a woman.

"Without doubt, all that Frances accomplished was the result of her faith, which always reigned fervently and vigorously in her heart; the human charity which inflamed her; and the constant prayer with which she penetrated to and obtained from God—with whom she was always closely joined—that which human weakness could not obtain.

"Even in the midst of the most assailing cares and anxieties of life, she strove and aimed toward this without permitting anything to turn her away—to please God and to work for His glory. To this end, nothing seemed for her laborious, nothing difficult, nothing beyond human strength aided by grace."

The feast day of Mother Cabrini is November 13, on which the Church prays: "O God, through the work of Saint Frances Cabrini you brought comfort and love to the immigrants and those in need. May her example and work be continued in the lives of those dedicated to You."

THÉRÈSE OF THE CHILD JESUS
(1873-1897)

THÉRÈSE was born January 2, 1873, in Alencón, France. Louis Martin, her father, and Zelie Guerin, her mother, had both aspired to the religious life in their youth, but God had other designs for them. He blessed their happy union with nine children. Of these, four died in their infancy, and five entered the cloister. The father and mother were worthy examples of true Christian parents. Every morning they assisted at Holy Mass; together they knelt at the Holy Table.

To be a spouse of Christ had been Thérèse's ardent desire since the early age of three. When she was nine and again when ten years old, she repeatedly begged to be received into the Carmel of Lisieux. On a pilgrimage to Rome with her father, she begged this favor of the Holy Father, Pope Leo XIII. "Well, my child, you will enter it if it be God's will," responded Pope Leo.

Consecrated to Divine Love

When Thérèse had completed her fifteenth year, the door of the convent finally opened to her. There the superiors put her virtues to the sharpest test. On January 10, 1889, she was invested with the holy habit and received the name Sister Thérèse of the Child Jesus and of the Holy Face. She pronounced her holy vows on September 8, 1890, and with all the fervor of her naturally ardent temperament, she gave herself to the practice of the interior life. On the path of spiritual childhood, of love and confidence, she became a great saint.

Thérèse's zeal for the conversion of sinners and for the sanctification of priests—the special aim of the Carmelite vocation—became more and more fervent as she tasted of the chalice of the Passion. She suffered much during her life, but it was hidden suffering. She writes: "I know of one means only by which to attain perfection: Love! Let us love, since our heart is made for nothing else. We must adhere to this simple and only word: Love. I will that creatures should not possess a single atom of my love. I wish to give all to Jesus, since He makes me understand that He alone is perfect happiness. All shall be for Him, all, and for Him alone!"

"The good God," she said, "does not need years to accomplish His work of love in a soul. Love can supply for length of years. Jesus, because He is eternal, regards not the time, but only the love." And love, indeed, did supply for years in Thérèse's case, for God took her in the springtime of her life, but by means of love she had, in that short space, attained a very high degree of sanctity.

Two of Thérèse's sisters had joined the Carmelite community previous to her entrance. Yet she seldom sought the pleasure of their companionship at recreation.

On the feast of the Most Holy Trinity, June 9, 1895, an interior inspiration urged her to consecrate herself to Divine Love as a sacrificial victim; that is, to offer herself to endure for love of God all sufferings and pains with which Divine Love desired to favor her. With these sentiments she bore all her interior and exterior trials, and God alone knows the extent of her sufferings.

Thérèse's Mission

Shortly before her death Thérèse said: "I feel that my mission is about to begin, my mission of bringing others to love our good God as I love Him, and teaching souls my little way of trust and self-surrender. I will spend my heaven in doing good upon earth." Her mission is to teach souls her way of spiritual childhood. She practiced all the virtues of childhood, but those which attracted her above all were the confidence and tender love which little ones show toward their parents. Love, confidence, and self-surrender are the keys to her spiritual life.

On September 30, 1897, Thérèse, the true victim of Divine Love, died of tuberculosis, a disease which in her case had assumed a very painful character. A moment before she died the patient sufferer once more made an act of perfect resignation, and with a loving glance at her crucifix, said, "Oh, I love Him! My God, I love You!" She was twenty-four years old when she died.

Sister Thérèse was canonized only twenty-eight years after her death. She was declared patroness of the Missions. Her feast day is celebrated on October 1, on which day the Church prays: "O God, who open your Kingdom to those who are humble and to little ones, lead us to follow trustingly in the little way of Saint Thérèse, so that through her intercession we may see your eternal glory revealed."

On October 19, 1997, Pope John Paul II proclaimed St. Thérèse the third woman Doctor of the Church.

MARIA GORETTI
(1890-1902)

MARIA was born of a poor family at Corinaldi, Italy, in 1890. Near Nettuno she spent a difficult childhood assisting her mother in domestic duties. She was of a pious nature and was often at prayer.

One afternoon in July, Maria was sitting at the top of the stairs of her cottage, mending a shirt. She was not quite twelve years old. A cart stopped outside, and a neighbor, Alessandro, eighteen years old, ran up the stairs. He seized her and pulled her into a bedroom. She struggled and tried to call for help, gasping that she would be killed rather than submit. "No, God does not wish it. It is a sin. You would go to hell for it." Alessandro began striking at her blindly with a long dagger.

Maria was taken to a hospital and suffered there for two days. When the priest asked her if she would forgive her murderer, she said, "Yes, I forgive him for the love of Jesus . . . and I want him to be with me in heaven. May God forgive him!"

Martyrdom

She died about twenty-four hours after the attack, kissing the crucifix and holding a medal of Our Lady. This happened in 1902.

Her murderer was sentenced to thirty years in prison. For a long time he was unrepentant. One night he had a dream of Maria, gathering flowers and offering them to him. His life changed. When he was released after twenty-seven years, his first act was to go to beg the forgiveness of Maria's mother.

Devotion to the young martyr grew, miracles were worked, and in less than a half-century she was canonized. At her beatification in 1947, her mother (then eighty-two), two sisters and a brother appeared with Pope Pius XII on the balcony of Saint Peter's. Three years later, in 1950, 66-year-old Alessandro

Serenelli knelt among the quarter-million people and cried tears of joy.

A Lesson To Be Learned

In the homily at the canonization of Maria Goretti in 1950, Pope Pius XII said: "The life of this modest girl not only is worthy of heaven but also calls for our admiration and veneration. It can teach parents to educate their children—who are gifts of God—in righteousness, in holiness, and in courage so that those children may live in accord with the precepts of the Catholic religion. In this way, when their virtue is tested, they will emerge victorious and untarnished thanks to the help of Divine grace.

"Maria's life can also teach innocent children and life-loving youth not to give in to vain and passing pleasures and the deceits of vice. May they instead aspire to Christian perfection even in the most difficult times. With the assistance of God's grace, all of us can one day attain this perfection if we assiduously apply ourselves to work and prayer.

"Assuredly, not all of us are called to suffer martyrdom; but we are called to possess Christian virtue. And virtue requires a courage that even if it does not reach the heroism of this girl nonetheless entails a continuous, constant, and diligent commitment until death. This commitment constitutes nothing less than a slow and continual martrydom, to which the Lord summons us: "The Kingdom of heaven suffers violence and the violent will possess it."

May all of us, aided by God's grace and encouraged by the example of Maria Goretti, endeavor to reach that goal. And from heaven where she enjoys eternal bliss, may this holy Virgin and Martyr obtain this grace for us from our Divine Redeemer by her intercession."

The feast day of Maria Goretti is July 6, on which day the Church prays: "O God, Author and Lover of chastity, You conferred on Saint Maria Your handmaid the grace of martyrdom at a youthful age. Through her intercession grant us constancy in Your commandments, You who gave the crown to a virgin who fought for You."